THE HISTORY OF
BRITISH VEGETATION

Modern Biology Series

General Editor
J. E. Webb, Ph.D., D.Sc.
Professor of Zoology,
Westfield College, University of London

HORMONES AND EVOLUTION
E. J. W. Barrington, M.A., D.Sc., F.R.S.

SPIDERS AND OTHER ARACHNIDS
Theodore Savory, M.A., F.Z.S.

ENERGY LIFE AND ANIMAL ORGANISATION
J. A. Riegel, Ph.D.

MICROBIAL AND MOLECULAR GENETICS
J. R. S. Fincham, Ph.D., Sc.D.

WOODLANDS
J. D. Ovington, Ph.D., D.Sc.

THE HISTORY OF BRITISH VEGETATION
W. Pennington, B.Sc., Ph.D.

ECOLOGY OF FUNGI
R. K. Robinson, M.A., D.Phil.

PHOTOSYNTHESIS
G. E. Fogg, Sc.D., F.R.S.

The History of
BRITISH
VEGETATION

WINIFRED PENNINGTON, B.Sc., Ph.D.
(Mrs. T. G. Tutin)
Department of Botany, The University, Leicester
and Freshwater Biological Association, Windermere

THE

Distributed in the United States by
CRANE, RUSSAK & COMPANY, INC. D
347 Madison Avenue
New York, New York 10017

ISBN 0 340 18667 4 Boards
ISBN 0 340 18666 6 Paper

First printed 1969
Second impression 1970
Second edition 1974

The English Universities Press Ltd.
St Paul's House, Warwick Lane, London EC4P 4AH

Text set in 11/12 pt. Monotype Plantin, printed by letterpress, and bound in Great
Britain at The Pitman Press, Bath

Preface

THIS small book is offered as an introduction to those two great classics of British botany, Professor Harry Godwin's "History of the British Flora", and the late Sir Arthur Tansley's "The British Islands and their Vegetation". It is hoped that those who read it will go on to study these larger works, on which the present book has drawn extensively for material.

Work on the history of British vegetation began in the 1930's, when Professor Godwin introduced into Britain the technique of pollen analysis of peats and Quaternary sediments. Under his leadership, in the Sub-department of Quaternary Research in the Cambridge Botany School, evidence was collected year by year as to the stages in forest history which had characterised each period of the Post-glacial. Later, investigations were extended back into Late-glacial, Full-glacial and Inter-glacial periods. Meanwhile, continual improvements in the technique of recognition of pollen grains provided for a more and more comprehensive analysis of the vegetation of each period. Professor Godwin, himself an ecologist, developed from the beginning the "ecological" interpretation of pollen diagrams, which emphasised the importance of reconstructing past plant communities, rather than the more limited, "geological" approach involved in regarding certain plants as zone-fossils. Research done under his influence also extended the investigation of "macroscopic" remains of plants in Quaternary deposits, following in the more geological tradition of earlier workers such as the Reids.

Now, thirty years after the beginning of Professor Godwin's pioneer work in Cambridge, there has been built up in Britain a great body of evidence on the history of many types of vegetation, so that in contemporary ecology and conservation, it is necessary to take into account the past as well as the present. The history of British vegetation is a subject which crosses departmental and faculty boundaries, for it links in a common interest biologists, geographers, geologists, archaeologists and local historians. This book has grown out of a course given to students in the University of Leicester, a course which has attempted to integrate Quaternary palaeobotany and stratigraphy with taxonomy and ecology, and during which questions have been discussed which covered ground shared with the departments of Archaeology and English Local History. In these days of specialisation, it has been satisfying to be concerned with such a many-sided subject.

I am very grateful to Professor Godwin, not only for my initial training in this discipline, but for many years of encouragement, and for permission to quote extensively from his works. I also acknowledge with gratitude my indebtedness to those friends with whom I have discussed particular problems, some of whom have allowed me to reproduce figures from their published work: Dr D. D. Bartley, Miss Clare Fell, Professor G. F. Mitchell, Professor F. Oldfield, Dr Judith Turner, Dr R. G. West and Mrs Gay Wilson. To my husband I am grateful, not only for continued encouragement without which the book would never have been finished, but for advice on nomenclature which ensured that the plant names used in this book are in conformity with the current (Second) edition of Clapham, Tutin and Warburg's "Excursion Flora of the British Isles."

The photographs which form the plates have nearly all been provided by other biologists, to whom I give my thanks. The majority were taken by Dr M. C. F. Proctor, to whom especial thanks are due; others are the work of Mr J. E. Raven, Mr J. E. Lousley, Dr J. Morton Boyd, and Miss N. J. Gordon. Dr J. K. S. St Joseph provided the air photograph which forms Plate 3; and the Geological Museum the reconstruction in Plate 1; both of these are Crown Copyright, and permission to reproduce them is gratefully acknowledged. To Messrs Collins I am grateful for permission to borrow and reproduce the photographs which form Plates 23, 24, 25, 26, 27 and 30, all of which have appeared in volumes of the New Naturalist series; for permission to use that in Plate 30 I am grateful also to Sir Edward Salisbury.

Because of different usages of the term "Zone", I should make it clear that in this book the usage is the same as that found in Professor Godwin's "History of the British Flora"—that is, a zone is regarded as having approximately synchronous boundaries in North-west Europe, so that it is permissible to use, for instance, "Zone 1", as a convenient name for an interval of time. This, of course, is contrary to that definition of a zone which states that it is a biostratigraphic unit only.

WINIFRED PENNINGTON.

Preface to the Second Edition

In the years since first publication so much new work has appeared that extensive additions and alterations have become necessary. This book remains as an introduction only—it has been impossible in a volume of this size to include reference to all the information on British vegetation history which is now available.

WINIFRED PENNINGTON.

Contents

1 The geological record: the Tertiary period in Europe

The present British flora

ALL history must begin somewhere. One natural starting-point for the history of British vegetation would be the time, about 5500 B.C., when Great Britain was cut off by the rising sea level from the continent of Europe, for the first time since the latest of the great glacial episodes—that one which came to an end between 8000 and 9000 B.C. During the years between the end of glacial conditions and about 5500 B.C., Great Britain was wide open to immigration of plants from neighbouring parts of the continental mainland. Species which we know to have been growing in Britain between the last glacial episode and 5500 B.C. are regarded as unquestionably native. After the marine transgression of about this date severed Britain from the continental mainland, there were comparatively few natural means of dispersal capable of carrying plants across the sea barrier. Species which had not reached Britain by 5500 B.C., and are now present, have mainly come as either deliberate or accidental introductions by the successive waves of human immigrants, beginning with the Neolithic peoples at about 3000 B.C. Some species appear to have failed by a narrow margin to reach Britain; any observant Briton travelling beyond Calais might wonder why that handsome conspicuous plant of French chalk fens and damp roadside habitats, *Cirsium oleraceum*, is absent from similar habitats outside Dover. The comparative poverty of the British flora, compared with that of continental Europe in comparable latitudes, is the result of successive wiping-out of frost-sensitive species by the repeated glacial episodes of the last million years. After each glacial period, with its wholesale extinction of plants from Britain, migrating plants, and animals, followed northwards in the footsteps of the retreating ice, and combined with the descendants of hardy species which had survived, to re-establish the British flora and fauna.

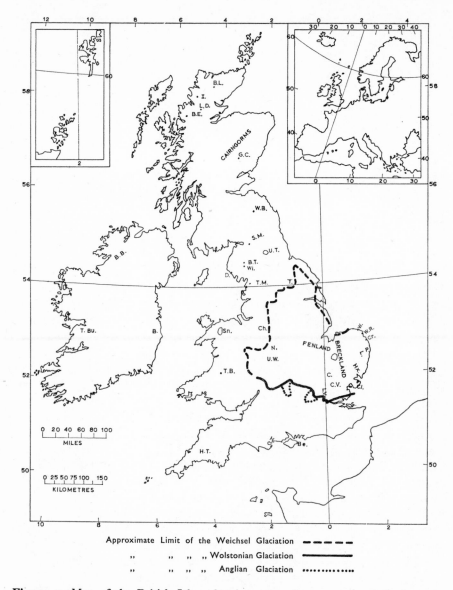

Approximate Limit of the Weichsel Glaciation ▬ ▬ ▬ ▬ ▬

　　　　,,　　　　　,,　　　,,　　,, Wolstonian Glaciation ▬▬▬▬▬

　　　　,,　　　　　,,　　　,,　　,, Anglian Glaciation ••••••••••••

Figure 1. Map of the British Isles, showing most places mentioned in the text.

KEY. B. = Ballybetagh, B.B. = Ben Bulben, Be = Bembridge, B.E. = Ben Eighe, B.L. = Ben Loyal, B.T. = Blelham Tarn, C. = Cambridge, Ch = Chelford, Cl = Clacton, Cr = Cromer, C.V. = Colne Valley, D. = Drigg, G.C. = Glen Clova, H. = Hordle, Hx. = Hoxne, H.T. = Hawk's Tor, I. = Inverpolly, L. = Ludham, L.D. = Loch Droma, L.V. = Lea Valley, N. = Nechells, P. = Pakefield, S. = Sheppey, Sn. = Snowdonia, S.M. = Scaleby Moss, T. = Tadcaster, T.B. = Tregaron Bog, T.Bu. = The Burren, T.M. = Thrang Moss, U.T. = Upper Teesdale, U.W. = Upton Warren, W. = Weybourne, Wi. = Windermere, W.B. = Whitrig Bog, W.R. = West Runton.

No attempt has been made to represent the positions of the ice-margins in Ireland, Scotland and Wales where these are still controversial.

For a more detailed map of the limits of ice advances in the British Isles, see Sparks & West, 1972, Fig. 5.18.

Geological Period			Central Europe (Probable correlations with Alpine glaciations)	N.W. Europe & Scandinavia	Britain
			HOLOCENE (Recent	Flandrian Interglacial	Post-glacial peat and sediments
QUATERNARY	PLEISTOCENE	RECENT	Würm Glaciation	Weichsel Glaciation	Many Late-glacial sites Barnwell Station and Lea Valley Arctic Beds Chelford Interstadial
				Eemian Interglacial	"Last" Interglacial Ipswich, Trafalgar Square
			Riss Glaciation	Saale Glaciation	Wolstonian Glaciation
			"Great" Interglacial	Holstein Interglacial	Hoxnian Interglacial
			Mindel Glaciation	Elster Glaciation	Anglian Glaciation
				Cromerian Interglacial	Cromer Forest Bed Series
			? Gunz Glaciation ? Donau Glaciation	Tiglian Interglacial = ? Pretiglian cold period	Complex pre-Cromerian sequence of probably three cold periods with intervening milder periods, in East Anglian deposits, including upper Crags.
TERTIARY					Coralline Crag in East Anglia
			Kroskienko flora (Poland)		
			PLIOCENE		
			Reuverian flora (Netherlands)		Plant beds in Derbyshire
			MIOCENE Alpine mountain-building		
			OLIGOCENE		Bembridge Beds
			EOCENE		Hordle Beds London Clay

Figure 2. Geological correlation table.
(For approximate time scale, see Fig. 3)

Each glacial episode was accompanied by a eustatic—that is, world-wide—fall in sea level, because so much water became locked up in the expanded ice-caps that a reduction in volume of the sea took place. This eustatic fall in sea level is known to have left a wide land bridge between England and Europe at the close of the last glaciation, and almost certainly this happened at the close of preceding glacial episodes. But as the sea level rose, with the return to the sea of melt-water from the ice-caps at the beginning of each interglacial, so Great Britain must have been cut off, each time, from plants migrating northwards from their southerly refuges. Plants extinguished by the severity of the climate of the glacial periods did not always succeed in returning by migration; the rhododendron is not regarded as a native plant in Britain today, though it reproduces and spreads luxuriantly under present climatic conditions, but the pollen of *Rhododendron ponticum* has been found in Ireland in sediments of at least one interglacial period.

For a full understanding of the climatic changes and plant migrations which led up to the state of the British flora and vegetation at the time of severance from the Continent, at about 5500 B.C., it is necessary to consider the course of events from, at least, the maximum of the previous glacial episode, and to relate this to the sequence of events in the whole Quaternary period—that is, the last one to two million years. For an even fuller understanding of the history of British vegetation, it is necessary to consider briefly the stages by which the "modern"—that is, Pleistocene—flora of Europe was developed from the very different vegetation of the Tertiary period—see the tables in Figs. 2 and 3. Near the beginning of the Tertiary, about 60 million years ago, many

			Age in years, *beginning of each period*
C E N O Z O I C	QUATERNARY	Post-glacial (Holocene)	10,000
		Pleistocene	1,000,000 to 2,000,000
	TERTIARY	Pliocene	*c.* 12,000,000
		Miocene	*c.* 28,000,000
		Oligocene	*c.* 38,000,000
		Eocene	60,000,000 to 70,000,000

Figure 3. Approximate time-scale.

plants whose relations today inhabit the tropical lowlands of Indo-Malaya were growing not far from Sheppey in south-east England. We know this because fragments of these plants, particularly their fruits and seeds, which can readily be identified, occur in great quantities in the London Clay which forms the low cliffs and the foreshore at Sheppey.

Research into plant history

The investigation of past floras through their fossil remains is carried out by the techniques of the palaeobotanist, but in Tertiary, and still more in Quaternary deposits, these techniques are different from those of palaeobotanists who work on older and harder rocks. From the softer Tertiary beds, plant remains where present can often be removed entire. Usually fruits and seeds and entire leaves are used as a basis of identification, but other anatomical structures, such as rose prickles, have been used to identify plants to genera and even species level, by comparison with living material. The techniques of "palynology" are concerned with the recognition of spores and pollen grains. Since the reproductive structures of plants form the basis of taxonomy, these are the parts of plants most readily identified, to family, genus, or species level, so it is not surprising that palynology and the identification of fruits and seeds have proved to be the most rewarding lines of investigation of the vegetation of the more recent past.

Study of "macroscopic" plant remains includes recognition of fruits, seeds, leaves, stems, etc., as distinct from the "microscopic" technique of palynology, and recognition of macroscopic remains provides factual evidence for the presence of the plants identified, within a distance from the site equivalent to, at least, the normal dispersal range of that fruit or seed. This is in contrast to the type of evidence provided by palynological investigation, because the dispersal range of pollen grains and spores is so much greater. Some pollen grains have been collected over the Atlantic, many hundreds of miles from land, so that the presence of an isolated pollen grain is not in itself proof of the local presence of a plant. Most pollen grains and spores, however, seem to reach the ground within quite a short distance of the plant which produced them, so most of the pollen identified from a Tertiary or Quaternary sediment or peat was probably produced by the local vegetation. The very large quantity in which these microfossils are found in most organic deposits means that their relative proportions provide much information about the *type* of vegetation which produced that particular "pollen rain", so that palynology can tell us more about past vegetations, whereas identification of macroscopic plant remains gives more certain information about the past distribution of a particular plant.

But in the general problem of attempting to reconstruct past vegetations, it is desirable to bear in mind the necessarily very fragmentary nature of both types of evidence. In the past as in the present, the normal fate of all parts of a dead plant was eventual destruction by the soil microflora and fauna, either directly or after ingestion, digestion and excretion by herbivorous animals. The particular importance of pollen grains and spores as microfossils is that the sporopollenin forming the outer coat is extremely resistant to decomposition by very many of these micro-organisms. There are no known anaerobic micro-organisms which can cause decay of the outer coat of pollen and spores, so that in a rapidly growing sediment, or in anaerobic water or peat, nearly all the pollen grains, and spores of ferns, horsetails, *Sphagnum* and so forth, which fall on to the surface, will be preserved. So in regions which contain either lakes with accumulating sediments, or growing peat bogs, a continuous record of the pollen-and spore-producing vegetation is built up, and changes in type of vegetation are recorded. From palynological analysis of a great many profiles from fen and bog peats and lake sediments, a fairly detailed picture is emerging of the changing vegetation during the last 10,000 years of Ireland, the East Anglian and Fen country lowlands, and the Highland zone of Great Britain, from Dartmoor to the Scottish Highlands—but there is still comparatively little direct evidence for vegetation history in the chalk and oolite areas of south-eastern England, because of the absence of sites yielding long profiles of peat or lake sediments. The study of pollen preserved in soil is in a comparatively early stage, and clearly it will never provide complete conformable evidence for vegetation changes as does a growing deposit. The conditions under which pollen grains and spores are, or are not, decomposed by micro-organisms in an aerobic soil, are as yet very incompletely understood.

The preservation of parts of plant bodies other than pollen or spores is largely dependent on their becoming incorporated in a watery medium or a fast-growing sediment, in which they are immediately protected from microbial decay and physical erosion. The importance of wet situations in the preservation of plant bodies from decay is reflected in the much greater knowledge we have of vegetation of those past periods when Britain had a predominantly wet surface and climate, such as the Carboniferous, compared with our scanty knowledge of the vegetation of predominantly desert periods, such as the Trias. This means that data from recognition of macroscopic plant remains are often "weighted" by the predominance of aquatic or peat-forming plants. Some of the best-known of Tertiary floras, including that of the Eocene London Clay, were identified from deposits which represent the debris deposited by large rivers on entering an estuary or lake. The plants identified from such an assemblage represent several distinct vegetation types, the plant remains being fortuitously brought together by conditions of topography, erosion and deposition, but still numerically dominated by riverside plants.

When it is realised that no more than a dozen or so areas in Europe have yielded deposits at all rich in samples of the Tertiary flora and vegetation, that is, of the vegetation which clothed Europe for about 60,000,000 years, then the extremely fragmentary nature of the fossil record is apparent. By contrast, the vegetation of Britain and continental Europe through the vicissitudes of the changing climates of the million or so years of the Quaternary period is comparatively well known, but closer study only serves to emphasise the inadequacy of the fossil record, and the still enormous gaps in our knowledge.

The Tertiary vegetation of Britain

Of the vegetation of Britain during this 60,000,000 years, only a few samples of any extent are as yet known. The Lower Eocene flora of the London Clay has been described in a monograph by Reid and Chandler, based largely on material exposed in the coastal beds at Sheppey. The same authors have identified somewhat smaller assemblages of plants from the Upper Eocene beds exposed in a coastal section at Hordle, near Bournemouth, and from the Oligocene beds at Bembridge in the Isle of Wight. Recently, attention has been directed to the Tertiary leaf-bearing beds of Mull, where the great Alpine mountain-building movements which culminated during the Miocene, caused cracking of the hard ancient rocks, and upwelling, through the cracks, of great basaltic lava flows. The leaf-bearing beds of Mull are interbedded with lava flows and as yet their exact age is uncertain. In sink holes in the limestone plateau of Derbyshire are clays containing pollen and spores of Miocene-Pliocene age. Older text-books put the Cromer Forest Bed of East Anglia into the Upper Pliocene, but the 18th Geological Congress in 1949 fixed the upper limit of the Pliocene (and hence of the Tertiary) at a horizon within the Crag succession of East Anglia, well below the Cromer Forest Bed, see Fig. 2.

The London Clay Flora can be seen in imaginative reconstruction in a painting at the Geological Museum: see Plate 1. The list of genera and species identified by Reid and Chandler suggests a tropical lowland evergreen forest, of a type now found in the Indo-Malayan region of South-east Asia. In this vegetation palms predominate, as indicated by the abundance of fossil fruits of the palm *Nypa*. *Nypa* is found today growing in brackish water along the estuaries of South-east Asia. Of the genera recognised from the London Clay flora, 73 per cent have living relations in the Malayan islands, and of the families represented, 11 per cent of the total are entirely tropical, and a further 32 per cent are almost entirely tropical, like the Palmae. Because of the conditions of deposition, it is virtually certain that these tropical plants must have grown within about a hundred miles of Sheppey. Their good state of preservation suggests an origin not far away, and the known facts of Tertiary geography rule out any suggestion that the plant remains could have originated in latitudes far to the south, in the present tropical belt. It seems that the Sheppey plant remains represent the debris reaching the sea at the mouth of a tropical river, under conditions comparable with the offshore drift to be seen today in New Guinea. A second element in the plant list, of which *Magnolia* is typical, is of woody plants of warm-temperate rather than sub-tropical climates, and is equally exotic to the present British flora. This type of plant probably came from higher altitudes than the coastal lowlands where *Nypa* was dominant. Though the London Clay plant assemblage includes several different types of vegetation, it establishes the flora of the Lower Eocene in Britain as bearing no resemblance at all to the modern European flora.

The Hordle flora from the Upper Eocene shows the beginning of the progressive change in flora and vegetation which characterised the Tertiary period. Most of the lowland tropical plants of the Indo-Malayan element of the London Clay flora have gone (*Nypa* being one of the few survivors) and woody plants of the warm-temperate *Magnolia* type make up most of the list, which suggests a vegetation resembling that of the mountains of Burma, West China, Japan and the Himalaya at present. Eight of the genera recognised have species now living in Britain, including the pine (*Pinus*) and pondweed (*Potamogeton*)—though the remains of these do not correspond with any living *species*.

The Bembridge beds of the Isle of Wight Oligocene have also yielded a plant list of a predominantly warm-temperate type, containing, along with palms and lianes of South-east Asian affinities, twelve genera with species now living in Britain, including *Pinus* and the poppy (*Papaver*).

The progressive changes in climate and vegetation throughout the Tertiary period are better illustrated by Pliocene deposits from the Continent. Both in the Reuverian flora from Limburg in the Netherlands, and in the Pliocene floras of southern Poland described by Szafer, there are many species now found in the mountains of West China, East Tibet and Japan, but also many species typical of the modern European flora. These include a spruce (*Picea*) and the hornbeam (*Carpinus betulus*). In the deposits at Krościenko in Poland appear also the characteristic trees of the European late-Tertiary forests—the wingnut (*Pterocarya*), the tulip-tree (*Liriodendron*) and the hemlock (*Tsuga*). These three trees, all native in North America or Asia, were extinguished from the European flora by the climatic changes which followed the end of the Tertiary period, but of course they grow and flourish well where planted, at least in southern Britain, today—see Fig. 4. In the later deposits at Mizerna in southern Poland, Szafer traced the further changes towards the modern European flora, with the development of forests of oak, and, at presumably higher altitudes, conifers including pines, spruces, firs (*Abies*) and hemlock. Among the warm-temperate trees found at Mizerna were the hickory (*Carya*) and the walnut (*Juglans*), as well as *Pterocarya*, and among other warmth-demanding plants was *Magnolia*.

Boulter's plant list from the Derbyshire sink holes, of Miocene-Pliocene age, includes the Tertiary genera *Sciadopitys* and *Liquidambar*, in addition to *Juglans*, *Carya* and *Tsuga*, with *Abies* and *Picea* and many genera still native to Britain, including *Pinus*, *Ulmus*, *Corylus*, *Alnus* and quercoid pollen. Szafer's findings in Poland provide the main evidence to show that by Upper Pliocene times, the East Asiatic species were disappearing from the European flora, and the percentage of genera belonging to the modern mid-European and Eurasiatic genera groups was steeply rising, so that at the opening of the Quaternary period, there were comparatively few genera present which are not now represented in the European flora.

Figure 4. *Pterocarya fraxinifolia*, a Tertiary relic, no longer native to Britain Reproduced by permission of Cambridge University Press, from the Guide to the Cambridge Botanic Garden.

The extinction of the genera now exotic in Europe was brought about by the considerable climatic deterioration which occurred at the time now fixed as the Pliocene/Pleistocene, and therefore Tertiary/Quaternary, boundary. In the British geological succession, this horizon is represented by a change in the Crag succession in East Anglia. The Crags are shelly marine deposits, formed under what appear to have been estuarine or shallow-marine conditions in the East Anglian area, and subsequently raised above the level of the sea so that they are now exposed in coastal sections in East Anglia. Their fossils are all animal, and include corals, molluscs and Foraminifera. The uppermost Pliocene bed, the Coralline Crag, was apparently formed under warm-temperate conditions, and a considerable diminution in temperature, revealed by change in species of Foraminifera and molluscs, marks the transition to the overlying Red Crag, the basal Pleistocene deposit. In Poland, at the corresponding horizon—that is, the Pliocene/Pleistocene boundary, the disappearance of the relatively warmth-demanding species *Carya tomentosa* and *Magnolia Cor* (Szafer) from the flora is also interpreted as indicating a fall in temperature.

As yet it has not been possible to correlate the British Crag succession in any detail with deposits of similar age on the Continent, but in both areas a marked cooling of climate represents the final phase in the transition which took place within the course of the Tertiary, from the tropical conditions and flora of the Eocene to the "modern" climate and flora at the opening of the Quaternary, that is, at the end of the Pliocene. Within the period represented by the Crags occurred a decrease in Pliocene forms of larger animals, such as the mastodons, and an increase in typically Pleistocene forms including elephant and horse.

The cooling climate of the Tertiary/Quaternary transition is of course known from evidence other than fossils. Penck and Bruckner, working on the glacial deposits and river terraces of the Alpine region, established that there had been during the Quaternary period four main phases of expansion of the Alpine glaciers on to the surrounding plains, and had given the names Gunz, Mindel, Riss and Würm to these glaciations. An earlier glaciation recognised in south-central Europe, the Donau glaciation, may belong to the close of the Pliocene, very possibly correlating with a cold period at this horizon described by Szafer within the vegetation succession at Mizerna in Poland. During the last twenty years, a period of rapidly increasing knowledge of British Pleistocene sequences, it has become apparent what problems may arise from premature correlations with Penck and Bruckner's Alpine sequence. "One particular difficulty was the desire to force the British sequence into the framework of glacials and interglacials described by Penck and Bruckner with reference to the Alps, which resulted in unsatisfactory correlations" (Sparks & West 1972).

2 Britain and Europe during the Quaternary glaciations

The early Pleistocene vegetation

THE coastal exposures of the Crags in East Anglia do not contain pollen or other plant remains; the evidence for climatic deterioration near the base of the marine Crag sequence was first found in changes in species of molluscs, indicative of a marked cooling of sea water early in the time-span represented. Within the last twenty years work on pollen grains and Foraminifera found in deep boreholes through the Crags at sites inland from the coast has established a sequence of stages for the Lower Pleistocene in the Crag basin (West 1968). These, based on vegetation changes deduced from pollen analysis, have been correlated with earlier descriptions of the Crags (Fig. 8), and quantitative studies of Foraminifera, which are useful temperature indicators (Funnell 1960, 1961) have confirmed West's interpretation of changes in pollen spectra as the results of climatic oscillations from temperate to cool and then back to temperate. Pollen spectra made up wholly or largely of tree pollen indicate periods when a temperate climate allowed the growth of forest, and those in which the dominance of tree pollen is replaced by that of plants of heath or grassland are interpreted as indicative of periods of lower temperature. Within the Lower Pleistocene deposits of East Anglia there is as yet no record of plants which by their tolerance of very low temperatures would indicate a tundra type of vegetation. Thus the sediments of the boreholes at Ludham and other sites do not record actual glaciations in the North Sea basin, but fluctuations from forest to a type of oceanic heath and back to forest. The oceanic heath is interpreted as the result of a climatic change for the worse, which probably produced glacial conditions in more northerly latitudes. The pollen, in both forest and heath times, was preserved in these off-shore marine sediments, which were accumulating in an early Pleistocene estuary, probably centred near the present site of Norwich. The periods of forest coincide with the presence of warm-water animals, and in the sediments containing the pollen of heath plants there is a higher proportion of animals having a northern type of distribution. Therefore it is true to say that while in Britain there are no glacial deposits within the Lower Pleistocene, in the micro-fossils of this East Anglian estuary we have at least two periods of colder climate recorded. Of conditions in the rest of Britain during this time we have no evidence at all, probably because over much of Britain the deposits of this period were largely destroyed by the advancing ice of later glaciations. Evidence for a similar series of Lower Pleistocene oscillations has been found in boreholes from the Netherlands, but as yet differences between the respective floras preclude exact correlation with the British sequence.

West named the two Lower Pleistocene forest periods in the Ludham borehole section the Ludhamian and Antian stages respectively. Between them came the period of oceanic heath which he called the Thurnian cool period. After the Antian came the second period of heath, the Baventian. Above this in the Ludham borehole lie the deposits of another temperate period; in this the flora resembles that of the basal temperate stage of the overlying Middle Pleistocene succession which is recognised at coastal exposures at the type sites—Paston, Beeston and West Runton. In a subsequent borehole at Stradbroke, Suffolk, Pre-Ludhamian deposits rich in *Pinus* pollen have been found within the Red Crag: see Fig. 8.

The temperate forests recorded in the pollen of the Lower Pleistocene warm periods are mixed coniferous and deciduous, and the presence of both *Tsuga* and *Pterocarya* makes the vegetation different from that of any subsequent period in Britain. Comparison of West's pollen diagrams with those from Early Pleistocene interglacials on the Continent shows that the "Tertiary" elements in the forests are on the whole less well represented in Britain—i.e. *Carya* and *Sciadopitys* have not yet been found in these earliest interglacials in Britain. In the deposits of the Ludhamian period pollen of two species of *Tsuga* is frequent—*T. canadensis* and *T. diversifolia*. The dominant tree pollen is that of *Pinus,* and also present are alder (*Alnus*), birch (*Betula*), hornbeam (*Carpinus*), oak (*Quercus*), spruce (*Picea*) and elm (*Ulmus*). The Ludhamian is shown to have been a period of forests by the fact that non-tree pollen is sparse compared with the total of tree pollen. The sparse non-tree pollen is made up of that of grasses, ericaceous plants and members of the Chenopodiaceae. The last probably confirms the estuarine character of the sediments since chenopods are so characteristic of coastal, particularly salt-marsh, vegetation.

In the overlying sediments of the Thurnian cold episode, the proportions of grass and ericaceous pollens rise until they greatly exceed the tree pollen; much of the ericaceous pollen resembles that of crowberry (*Empetrum nigrum*), with ling (*Calluna*) and other genera represented. This treeless *Empetrum* heath represents a vegetation tolerant of more severe climatic conditions than is forest, and so the climatic change from the temperate

Ludhamian to the cold Thurnian is recorded. *Empetrum* heath is, however, characteristic of oceanic climate, so that though the Thurnian episode was cold, it was not continental in the region which is now Norfolk. Above the Thurnian, coniferous and deciduous forests similar to those of the Ludhamian appear to have become again the dominant vegetation; this second forest period is the Antian Interglacial. Above it, the Baventian cold period would appear to have been climatically more severe than the Thurnian, because evidence of permafrost appears for the first time in Baventian deposits. After this cold period, the characteristic Lower Pleistocene trees *Tsuga* and *Pterocarya* appear only separately and sparsely in the deposits of Middle Pleistocene temperate periods—*Tsuga* for the last time in the Pastonian, and *Pterocarya* only in the Hoxnian.

In North America, *Tsuga* and *Carya* have remained as members of the much richer native flora until the present day. The explanation would seem to be that in Europe the high mountain ranges run east-west (from the Pyrenees to the Carpathians) and so must have prevented the dispersal to more southerly latitudes, and subsequent return, of many of the more thermophilous species during each glacial episode of the Quaternary. In America, on the other hand, the high mountain ranges run north-south, and so there must have been free dispersal towards the equator during glaciations and then again towards the poles after the end of each glaciation. Consequently many more species were permanently extinguished from the European flora than from that of North America, and there are today very many more species of forest trees in North America than in northern Europe in comparable latitudes.

The Middle Pleistocene vegetation: (i) Pastonian, Beestonian and Cromerian

While pollen diagrams from the Lower Pleistocene temperate stages at Ludham cannot readily be subdivided (see West 1968, Fig. 13.4) all subsequent temperate stages show a sequence of pollen zones which can be related to environmental changes. The zones have a characteristic pattern which records a cycle of climatic amelioration and subsequent deterioration, and are used to subdivide all deposits of Middle and Upper Pleistocene temperate stages. They are defined by West as follows (the youngest first): see Fig. 6.

Zone IV (post-temperate) contains pollen indicative of a declining forest of undemanding trees and expanding heaths: *Betula, Pinus, Picea* and *Ericales* are characteristic types.

Zone III (late-temperate) contains pollen of trees which were not abundant earlier in the stage. In different stages this may be of *Tsuga* (Pastonian) *Picea* (Cromerian) *Abies* (Hoxnian) or *Carpinus* (Hoxnian and, particularly, Ipswichian).

Zone II (early temperate) contains an overwhelming dominance of pollen of trees of mixed oak forest—*Quercus, Ulmus, Fraxinus* and *Corylus*.

Zone I (pre-temperate) contains pollen of the pioneer forest trees *Betula* and *Pinus*, together with much pollen of shrubs and light-demanding herbs.

The sequence of Middle Pleistocene deposits from which has come the evidence for British vegetation history at this time is found on the Norfolk coast at West Runton near Cromer (see Fig. 5.6 in Sparks & West 1972). Exposed on the foreshore is solid Chalk, and above this on the beach a succession of Weybourne Crag, silts and sands. The overlying freshwater sands and muds, exposed at the base of the cliff, constitute the type section for the Cromerian, the earliest British interglacial stage, and the cliff itself is made of the till and contorted drift left by the first Quaternary ice in Britain, that of the Anglian (formerly called Lowestoft) glaciation. Within the uppermost Weybourne Crag and the tidal silts of this sequence is found evidence for the temperate Pastonian period, when mixed oak forest similar to that of today was present, but differed from that of later stages in that it was apparently invaded by *Tsuga* in Zone P III. Above this, sands and gravels with an Arctic flora and showing permafrost features record the Beestonian cold period which followed. In the overlying Cromerian deposits is a rich record of the Cromerian flora which, though apparently about 700,000 years old, closely resembles the contemporary British flora.

Cromerian deposits are present at many places along the coast, from Weybourne and Sheringham in Norfolk to Pakefield in Suffolk. Early work on their rich content of plant macroscopic remains, by Clement Reid, produced a long list of species records, of which only 5 per cent are not now present in the British flora. In the small group of exotic species four (*Picea abies, Trapa natans, Azolla filiculoides* and *Naias minor*) reappear in Britain in later interglacials, and *Corema intermedia* is now extinct.

Most of our present native trees have been identified from the Cromer Forest Bed—i.e. *Pinus*, yew (*Taxus*), *Quercus*, beech (*Fagus*), *Ulmus*, *Betula*, hazel (*Corylus*) and *Carpinus*. Among the herbaceous plants recorded by Clement Reid are many, e.g. *Stellaria media, Rumex acetosella*, and *Polygonum aviculare*, which are now regarded primarily as weeds of cultivation, because of their restriction to open ground. Their presence in the Cromer Forest Bed Series shows that during this interglacial there were sites where vegetation other than forest flourished, and that these plants were able to be efficiently dispersed before man could have played a part in their dispersal.

Figure 5 represents a schematic pollen diagram through deposits of the Cromerian interglacial, which as we have seen lies between Beestonian deposits (containing evidence in both pollen and permafrost for an Arctic environment in Norfolk—Cromer) and the Till of the Anglian glaciation. The freshwater deposits of the early Cromerian at West Runton are overlain by marine deposits of the Cromerian marine transgression. High sea levels were found in the middle of each interglacial at the time of maximum temperatures, when the world's ice caps were at minimum size and the volume of the oceans at its maximum. "Compared with the succeeding interglacials the Cromerian vegetational history is distinct in the absence or scarcity of *Hippopha* in the late-glacial zone, the very low frequencies of *Corylus* throughout, the high frequencies of *Ulmus* and scarcity of *Tilia* in zone C II, and the late phase, zone C III, with *Abies* and *Carpinus*." (West 1968, p. 305.) Unfortunately the exposures from which the species identifications were made from macroscopic remains, many years ago, no longer exist, and so it is not possible to know the position of these records relative to the horizons in the pollen diagram. "The Lower Freshwater Bed" of Clement Reid cannot be identified with certainty and so cannot be placed in the stratigraphic sequence described from West Runton. It was from this bed that the warmth-demanding water chestnut, *Trapa natans*, was identified. None of the characteristically Tertiary plants of the Lower Pleistocene has been recorded from the Cromerian; it seems clear that most of the impoverishment from the richer Pliocene flora had been completed before the onset of the first of the Quaternary glaciations of south-east Britain.

The Middle Pleistocene vegetation: (ii) The Anglian Glaciation and Hoxnian Interglacial

Above the Cromer Forest Bed lie the oldest glacial deposits of the British Quaternary sequence. The cliff at West Runton is made up in its lower part of fluviatile sands of an early glacial period and then of about 30 m of glacial deposits—Cromer Till and contorted drift. At Corton, near Lowestoft, the Cromer Forest Bed series in the base of the cliff is overlain by uncontorted glacial deposits consisting of two tills separated by the sandy Corton Beds, within which are silt lenses containing evidence of a cold flora, compatible with glacial conditions. The cliff section at Corton has been adopted as the type site for the first glacial stage, the Anglian.

The upper till at Corton is a chalky boulder clay—the Lowestoft Till. Chalky boulder clay is widespread in East Anglia, from Essex to North Norfolk, and no general agreement has been reached as to whether it represents the deposits of a single glacial stage or two. The map in Fig. 1 shows the limits of the East Anglian glacial deposits as the products of two successive glaciations, called by West (1963, 1968) the Lowestoft and Gipping glacial stages. These were separated by West on the basis of interglacial lake deposits found at several sites filling hollows or channels in the surface of the Lowestoft till, and named, from the type site in a brickyard at Hoxne, Suffolk, as deposits of the Hoxnian Interglacial. The organic Hoxnian lake muds are at no site covered by glacial deposits, but by solifluction material or cryoturbated sands

formed under periglacial conditions. Since by measurements of stone orien-
tation in the East Anglian tills West had been able to distinguish two different
chalky tills, he correlated the periglacial deposits above the Hoxnian temperate
deposits with the upper of these tills, and equated this with the Gipping Till
of Baden-Powell. A Gipping glacial stage was therefore supposed to have
followed the Hoxnian temperate stage, and to have spread glacial deposits
southwards almost to the Thames. This is now questioned by some geologists,
who can find no evidence on which to subdivide the East Anglian Chalky
Boulder Clay. The age of the boulder clay is therefore still in question.
Since it lies between the temperate deposits of two quite distinct interglacials
(above the Cromerian at Corton and below the Hoxnian at Hoxne and at
Marks Tey, Essex) it must on biological evidence date from the glacial stage
between them. On biological correlations with the Continental sequence,
based on the similarity between plant and animal remains in the East Anglian
interglacials and those found at interglacial sites in north-west Europe, this
glacial stage would be the Elster (Tab. 2), with which the Anglian is therefore
correlated by Sparks and West (1972). Some geomorphologists, however,
can find good reason for supposing that the East Anglian Chalky Boulder
Clay must be more recent, and would correlate it with the Continental Saale
(Tab. 2). The succession in East Anglia therefore remains controversial.

The vegetation history of the Hoxnian interglacial has been worked out
quite fully by pollen analysis of lake sediments at Hoxne by Dr R. G. West
and at Marks Tey by Dr C. Turner: see Fig. 6, and Fig. 13.8 in West (1968)
Its characters include an abundance of the shrub *Hippophaë* in the pre-
temperate stage, the presence of *Taxus* in the mixed oak forest of the early
temperate stage, and of *Abies*, *Picea* and *Carpinus* in the late temperate stage,
together with small amounts of the "Tertiary relic" *Pterocarya*, which appears
to have been present for the last time in Western Europe at this time. The
water fern *Azolla filiculoides*, now found native only in the Americas, also
appears for the last time in the British flora. In Irish deposits of Hoxnian age
is found pollen of *Rhododendron ponticum* (nearest native station now Central
Portugal) and remains of several ericaceous plants now characteristic of the
highly oceanic Lusitanian flora of South-west Ireland, including *Erica
mackiana* and *Daboecia cantabrica*. These records, and the abundance of
Ilex pollen, suggest a highly oceanic climate.

From both the Hoxne brickpit and from deposits of Hoxnian age at Clacton-
on-Sea have come what are probably the oldest human tools in Britain—
hand-axes belonging to the Acheulian culture of the Lower Palaeolithic.
At Hoxne these flint artifacts occur in zone IId of the pollen diagram (Fig. 6),
and coincide with a temporary vegetation change reflected in a marked expansion of grassland and herbaceous vegetation at the expense of trees of the dry
land, alder not being affected. A similar episode is recorded at a comparable
horizon at Marks Tey, where teeth of *Elephas antiquus* were present within

the phase of high non-tree pollen. Though the effects of deliberate forest clearance by man are now widely recognised in pollen diagrams from the Early Neolithic period on (Chap. 7) it is difficult to interpret this episode in the very early history of man in Britain. At Marks Tey Dr Turner found charcoal within the open-water lake sediments, and suggested that an extensive forest fire could have caused the initial deforestation and that grazing pressure by large herbivores could explain why the forest was kept open for the 350 years recorded by the supposedly annual laminations in the Marks Tey sediments.

The Upper Pleistocene vegetation: (i) the Wolstonian Glaciation and Ipswichian Interglacial

Interglacial deposits of Hoxnian type and therefore age have been described from Nechells in the Midlands beneath thick sheets of the main till, which has therefore been identified as of post-Hoxnian age. The type site for the post-Hoxnian glacial stage is now at Wolston, Warwickshire, in the West Midlands, as described in the recent publication of the Geological Society of London—"A correlation of Quaternary deposits in the British Isles" by Professor Mitchell, Dr Penny, Professor Shotton and Dr West. This discusses the relative ages of the chalky boulder clay of the East Midlands and of East Anglia. The established facts are that there is biological evidence for a cold stage in East Anglia between the deteriorating climate shown by periglacial floras above the Hoxnian and the late-glacial floras found below the quite different temperate deposits of the most recent interglacial stage, the Ipswichian. It is the extent of glaciation within this cold phase which is controversial.

The last interglacial before the most recent glaciation is represented in Britain by plant-bearing beds from river terraces. The Ipswichian or Trafalgar Square Interglacial is firmly correlated with the Eemian Interglacial of North-west Europe, where again rising water levels formed a large inland sea, the Eem Sea. One of the localities for the deposits of this interglacial is in old deposits of the River Thames below parts of London, where from time to time these plant- and animal-bearing deposits—mainly river sands—are exposed in the excavations for foundations of new buildings. The deposits actually found beneath Trafalgar Square were from the middle warm period of this interglacial, when *Trapa natans*, *Acer monspessulanum*, and other plants now found only far to the south of Britain, were part of the British flora, and when *Elephas antiquus*, *Hippopotamus* and *Rhinoceros* were part of the fauna—see Fig. 9. The remains of molluscs and of beetles found in the Trafalgar Square sands also included many species characteristic of climates warmer than our present. The age of this flora and fauna is about 100,000 years; summer temperatures were probably 2 to 3°C higher than now.

At various sites in the Ipswich area, West and other workers have found

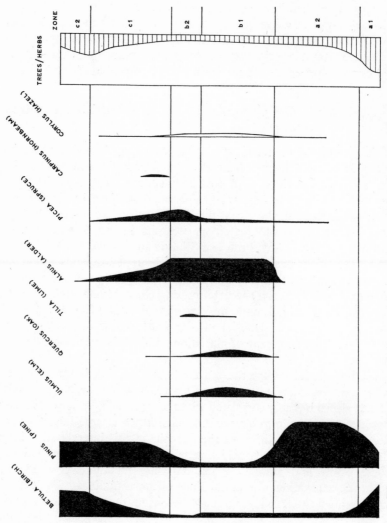

Figure 5. A schematic pollen diagram from the Cromerian Interglacial, after R. G. West.

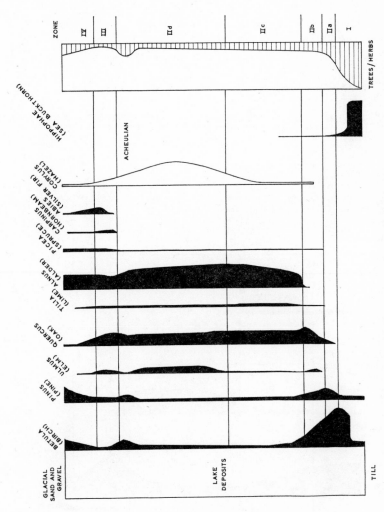

Figure 6. A schematic pollen diagram from the Hoxnian Interglacial, after R. G. West.

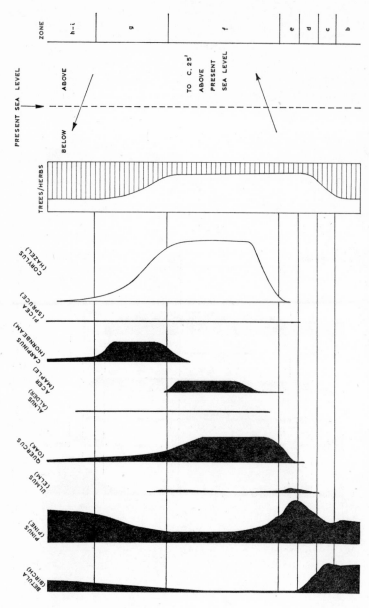

Figure 7. A schematic pollen diagram from the Ipswichian Interglacial, after R. G. West. Figures 5, 6 and 7 are reproduced, with permission, from R. G. West in *Proc. Linn. Soc. Lond.*, 172, 1961.

deposits which span the cycle of this interglacial, and agree in showing a high percentage of *Carpinus* pollen in the later stages of the mid-interglacial warm period, and some *Acer* pollen. *Tilia* and *Picea* are noticeably less well represented in this interglacial in Britain than in neighbouring parts of the Continent, and West suggests that this is because the sea level rose at an early stage in this particular interglacial, cutting off Britain from the Continent before *Tilia* and *Picea* had fully established themselves. *Abies* was not present in this interglacial and so forms a genus which was extinguished from the British flora by the preceding glacial phase, and failed to return subsequently. Chap. 10 in Sparks & West (1972) summarises the present state of knowledge of this interglacial.

Figures 5 to 7, reproduced from West's work by kind permission of the Linnean Society, show generalised pollen diagrams representing the vegetation succession during the three Quaternary interglacials. Each shows the characteristic cycle from a "late-glacial" stage, then conifer-birch forest, leading on to the mid-interglacial stage of mixed deciduous forest, and then after the "climatic optimum", a characteristic regression to a second coniferous forest stage and then towards a treeless vegetation in the early stages of

Ludham Borehole	*Sheringham-Mundesley* succession	*Crag succession*
	LOWESTOFT TILL	
	Cromerian (Cromer Forest Bed) *Temperate* — CROMER FOREST BED SERIES	
	BEESTONIAN *Cold*	
L5 = Upper Temperate Stage	Pastonian *Temperate*	
BAVENTIAN *Cold* End of *Tsuga & Pterocarya*		Weybourne Crag
Antian *Temperate*		Norwich Crag
THURNIAN *Cold*		
Ludhamian *Temperate* (Pre-Ludhamian elsewhere)		Red Crag
	PLIOCENE	Coralline Crag

Figure 8. A Correlation Table of Early and Middle Pleistocene vegetation stages in East Anglia, based on the work of R. G. West.

the next glaciation. Differences between the vegetation of successive inter-glacials are attributed partly to differences in details of the return to Britain by migration of the trees driven out by the previous glaciation, which depend partly on the rate of eustatic rise in sea-level in the first part of the interglacial cycle, and partly to some difference in the actual temperatures reached at the climatic optimum of each interglacial. For example, the flora and fauna of the Ipswichian Interglacial indicate that temperatures must have been higher in Southern England at the warmest period of this interglacial than they have been at any time in the Post-glacial period since the latest glacial episode, that is, in our present interglacial, the Flandrian. A reconstruction of the flora and fauna of the Thames valley during the Ipswichian (Trafalgar Square) Interglacial, is reproduced in Fig. 9.

Figure 9. "London 100,000 years ago", a reconstruction of the flora and fauna of the Trafalgar Square (Ipswichian) Interglacial. After an illustration, by permission: Copyright "The Illustrated London News".

3

The last Full-glacial period in Britain

Radiocarbon dating

FROM the break-up of the temperate plant communities of the last inter-glacial stage, through the vicissitudes of the most recent glaciation of Northern Europe and the ten thousand years since it ended, the student of vegetation history now has much more material evidence than was available for earlier periods. The superficial deposits which mantle so much of Britain contain unending stores of factual evidence which continue to come to light as new excavations reveal new sections and as modern methods of investigation are applied to older sections and natural exposures. Organic deposits of the last Full-glacial stage and younger deposits fall within the span of radiocarbon dating, which is about 70,000 years. On this basis the most recent glaciation of Britain is firmly correlated with the Weichselian of Northern Europe: the British stage name, recently adopted, is the Devensian, and the type site is at Four Ashes in Staffordshire. Radiocarbon dating of moss plants found beneath thick deposits of glacial till in East Yorkshire has shown that there the main till dates from less than 18,500 years ago.

When radiocarbon dating was first introduced it was assumed that the scale of years produced by measurement of the proportion of the carbon isotope ^{14}C (radiocarbon) remaining in organic material, followed by conversion to years elapsed since formation of the organic matter by calculation based on the known rate of decay of ^{14}C, gave a true scale of calendar (sidereal) years, since there was at that time no reason to suppose that the concentration of ^{14}C in the atmosphere had not been constant. Recently however the method of dendrochronology has made it possible to compare the time-scale provided by radiocarbon years with the time-scale of sidereal years obtained from counting the annual growth rings of certain long-lived trees, notably the bristle-cone pine (*Pinus aristata*) in North America. By calibration of identifiable sequences of rings of different widths it has been possible to extend even the

Plate 1. A reconstruction of the landscape in London Clay times. Geological Survey photograph, Crown Copyright—Reproduced by permission of the Controller of H.M. Stationery Office.

Plate 2. Naddle Forset Westmorland. A heavily grazed *Quercus petraea* woodland, with no regeneration of the oak.

Plate 3. Air photograph of Blelham Tarn and the surrounding woodland and pasture, North Lancashire. The woodland is mixed oak–alder–birch. Blelham Bog lies to the left of the tarn, in the upper part of the picture. Photograph by J. K. St Joseph, Cambridge University Collection. Reproduced by permission; Crown Copyright.

Plate 4. Highland pine forest, western type, at Coille na Glas Leitire, Beinn Eighe National Nature Reserve, Wester Ross. J. Morton Boyd.

Plate 5. Highland birch forest with alder in the foreground; Dundonnel Forest, Wester Ross. M. C. F. Proctor.

Plate 6. Birch-rowan wood on the island Eilean Mor in Loch Sionascaig, Inverpolly National Nature Reserve, Wester Ross. Cul Beag in background. Miss N. J. Gordon.

Plate 7. Malham Tarn, West Yorkshire. Marginal vegetation of *Phalaris* and *Filipendula* in the foreground; behind, raised bog to the left, and fen carr to the right. M. C. F. Proctor.

Plate 8. Pennine peat; Scar Close Moss, Chapel-le-Dale, with Ingleborough in the background. *Eriophorum vaginatum* (Sheathed Cotton sedge in fruit. M. C. F. Proctor.

Plate 9. Tregaron Bog, Cardiganshire. A complex of three raised bogs. In the growing peat there has been preserved a continuous record of the vegetation history of the surrounding land, in the form of pollen. M. C. F. Proctor.

Plate 10. Pine stumps now buried in blanket peat, near Slieve League, Co Donegal. M. C. F. Proctor.

long sequence counted from the wood of living trees by using yet older dead wood, so that a tree-ring chronology for the last 7000 years has been built up. Many radiocarbon dates have been obtained for rings of wood already dated by counting back from the present in the tree-ring chronology; comparison shows that the two methods of dating agree well over the last 2000 years, but then begin to diverge, the age in radiocarbon years being consistently too young (by up to 900 years at 5000 years ago) in comparison with the age in sidereal years given by the number of annual tree-rings. Since botanists are convinced that these rings represent a true record of the number of years in question, the discrepancy has been explained by supposing that the concentration of ^{14}C in the atmosphere, established by the cosmic ray flux, has not been constant. Support for the time-scale "corrected" by the tree-ring chronology has come from comparison of ^{14}C dates for archaeological material with the dates for that material on the Egyptian historical chronology, including astronomically verifiable Egyptian dates. Such comparisons agree better with the corrected date than with the age in radiocarbon years. Hence it has become customary to give dates within the last ten thousand years in "radiocarbon years ago" (B.P. indicating Before Present, Present being defined as A.D. 1950) rather than as calendar dates A.D. or B.C. The correction of the radiocarbon time-scale has been published (Suess 1970, see Fig. 9.3 in Sparks & West 1972). As yet there is no method available for independent dating of material more than 7,000 years old, so it is not known what correction should be applied to older dates.

Full-glacial deposits

At Wretton in Norfolk in the valley of the river Wissey, terrace deposits containing an Ipswichian flora are overlain by sands and gravels representing periglacial deposits of the cold stage which followed. Deposits of this cold period have been found at many other sites in Britain outside the limits of ice advance as recorded by its till—the "New Drift"—see Fig. 1. Conditions in the unglaciated south of Britain were at times clearly very severe, with evidence of periglacial soil disturbance and permafrost. But as more and more sites are investigated it becomes increasingly certain that for some of the 50,000 years of the last glacial period, rich biota flourished in southern Britain, and ideas prevalent fifty years ago that the British flora was temporarily almost exterminated by the severity of the last glaciation have now been completely abandoned.

It is now well established that the Full-glacial period included several interstadials—periods during which temperatures must have exceeded those of a glacial stage. To the palaeobotanist the most useful definition of an interstadial has been that which described it as indicative of non-glacial conditions but "either too short or too cold to permit the development of

temperate deciduous forest of the interglacial type in the region concerned"
(West 1968, p. 222).

Within the last fifteen years the study of Quaternary insect assemblages
by Dr G. R. Coope and his co-workers in Birmingham has shown that insects,
particularly beetles (Coleoptera) whose remains are often very abundant in
Quaternary deposits, adjusted their ranges markedly in response to environmental fluctuations. By interpreting climatic conditions at the time of formation of a deposit in terms of the present distribution of the species and species
assemblages of beetles in Europe and Asia, figures can be given for temperatures
which must have prevailed at the time of formation (Coope, Morgan & Osborne
1971).

The end of the Eemian (Ipswichian) Interglacial and onset of colder conditions at the opening of the Devensian (Weichsel) glaciation, falls approximately at the present limit of radiocarbon dating. Evidence of conditions in
Britain at approximately this time has been found in the gravels of the Intermediate Terrace of the River Cam, at Cambridge. In the excavation for
foundations of new university buildings at Sidgwick Avenue, a fossiliferous
deposit was found at the base of this gravel, and yielded macroscopic plant
remains (including those of bryophytes), remains of molluscs, Coleoptera, and
a skull of *Bison priscus*. Both plant remains and Mollusca showed that in-
habitants of several different types of habitat must have been present, some
from dry land, some from running water, some from pools, and some characteristic of open sands and gravels. No pollen was preserved in this material.
The interpretation which best fits the facts is—"If we envisage the accumulating terrace as traversed by a system of braided channels constantly shifting
about the undulating surface, it would provide the full variety of habitats
which our evidence seems to require"—Lambert (1963). The abundance of
shade-intolerant species, e.g. *Helianthemum canum* (Plate 19), means that
willows, the only woody plants recorded, must have been sparse, and many
plants now characteristic of mountains, screes, cliffs and shingle show that
there must have been well-drained, open habitats. Both plant species and
molluscs agree in suggesting cool to cold conditions, but a few southern species
of molluscs were present, and three of the plants—*Ajuga cf reptans*, *Potamogeton crispus* and *Groenlandia (Potamogeton) densus*, have a generally southern
range in Europe at the present day. A mixture such as this, of southern,
northern and Arctic-Alpine species, is more likely to be found late in an interglacial, with the southern forms either surviving in favourable places or being
secondarily derived from earlier deposits of the interglacial. On geomorpho-
logical grounds, the Sidgwick Avenue gravels, which lie on the Intermediate
Terrace of the Cam, would be expected to occupy a position intermediate in
time between the Histon Road deposits of the higher terrace, which are of
Ipswichian (Eemian) age, and the later deposits of the lower, Barnwell Station
Terrace, which have been dated to about 17,550 B.C.

	Zone	British Isles	Date	N.W. Europe
LATE-WEICHSELIAN (top)	III	Post-Alleröd cold period: corrie glaciers in the north, solifluction on Bodmin Moor	8,300 B.C. ⎫ 8,800 B.C. ⎭	Younger Dryas
	II	Alleröd Interstadial		Alleröd Interstadial
LATE-GLACIAL			10,000 B.C.	Older Dryas Bölling Interstadial
		Loch Droma organic silts	10,870 B.C.	
	I	Colney Heath erratics	11,600 B.C.	
		Blelham Bog kettlehole, organic mud	12,380 B.C.	
		Barnwell Station Beds	17,550 B.C.	
		Dimlington silts	18,500 Before Present	
FULL-GLACIAL (WEICHSELIAN)		Lea Valley Arctic Beds	28,000 Before Present	
		Fladbury	38,000 Before Present	
		Upton Warren	42,000 Before Present	
		Chelford Interstadial	60,000 Before Present	
		Sidgwick Avenue Beds		

Figure 10. A correlation and dating table of Devensian (Weichselian) and Late-Devensian deposits in Britain.

The glacial deposits of the Devensian stage constitute the "New Drift" (Fig. 1) a till which is largely of British derivation, carried south into the Vale of York and the Cheshire Plain by ice originating in the mountains of Scotland and the Lake District, and pushed eastwards by Welsh ice. At its maximum this ice reached the Escrick moraine in the Vale of York and to Smestow near Wolverhampton; within this drift limit no organic deposits are known from within the till and so no radiocarbon dates for the till are available. On the east coast from Hessle in Yorkshire to Hunstanton in Norfolk are boulder clays of foreign origin, attributed to the Scandinavian ice which impinged on to the British coast of the North Sea. At Dimlington in East Yorkshire, silts containing remains of the moss *Pohlia wahlenbergii,* cf. var. *glacialis,* which now lives in cold water habitats associated with snow beds and glaciers, lie beneath this till, and have been radiocarbon dated to *c.* 18,500 years B.P., thus assigning the till to the most recent period of the Weichselian glaciation, the Upper Pleniglacial. Coleoptera in the Dimlington Silts indicate very harsh climatic conditions. West of the Pennines, the till representing the most southerly position of the ice margin near Wolverhampton overlies organic material of Mid-Weichselian age at Four Ashes, and this ice advance is there dated to *c.* 25,000 years ago.

Devensian (Weichselian) interstadials

At Chelford in Cheshire a section exposed in a sand quarry shows a bed of peat, containing large tree trunks of pine, spruce and birch, beneath the sand and till of the main ice advance from the Irish Sea. The tree trunks gave a date of *c.* 60,000 years. The vegetation, as shown by pollen analysis of the peat layer, was a type of northern coniferous forest similar to that now found in parts of Finland; it is the latest record of the presence of *Picea* in the British flora. A very similar type of vegetation, dated to about 59,000 years ago, has been described from the Brørup Interstadial in Denmark, where the vegetation sequence has been revealed by pollen analysis of sediments of a lake which then existed below what is now a bog, at Brørup in West Jutland, outside the limit of the Weichsel glaciation of Denmark. Both the Chelford and the Brørup deposits therefore date from a climatic oscillation during the early part of the Weichsel glaciation, and record a time when the temperature in England and in Jutland permitted the development of coniferous forest with birch, but not the spread of more thermophilous trees. Therefore this oscillation was not of the magnitude of an interglacial. The abundant beetle fauna of the Chelford peat has been described by Coope, who reports that "The whole insect fauna could well occur today in and around a mossy pool in the eastern Scandinavian coniferous forest" (Coope, 1965).

A long period of cold climate followed the Chelford Interstadial, before the glacial maximum represented by the till at Chelford and the glacial deposits at Dimlington. Many organic deposits now known from the English Midlands date from this long cold period. The plant remains found within them are all alike in the absence of any trace of forest trees, either in macroscopic remains or in pollen percentages. On some definitions of an interstadial none represent interstadial floras. But the insect remains, intensively studied by Coope *et al.* (1971), show that the period can be divided into three—an initial cold phase, then a warm interlude, in which the Coleopteran assemblages indicate July temperatures of at least 15°C, and then a second cold period, with truly tundra conditions leading up to the glacial maximum—that recorded at Dimlington. It appears that Coleoptera can give a more precise record of the temperature oscillations within a glacial stage than can plants. This may reasonably be supposed to be because plants extinguished in Britain by the initial climatic severity—as the forest trees were extinguished after Chelford times—survived only in refuges far to the south. Amelioration of climate in mid-Weichselian times was apparently followed rapidly by movement of insects from their more southerly ranges, but plants disperse so slowly compared even with flightless insects that it is deduced that during the mid-Weichselian period of warmer climate no northward expansion of forest reached the English Midlands, though the climate there at that time would have permitted the growth of trees. This raises the question of whether interstadial climates can be deduced from plant evidence alone.

As yet there is only fragmentary evidence for vegetation changes following Chelford—Brørup time, as the climate deteriorated towards the cold conditions recorded by the presence of arctic beetles at Four Ashes in Staffordshire and Earith in Huntingdonshire. "Both these faunas represent truly tundra conditions with average July temperatures at or below 10°C (Coope *et al.* 1971).

The flora and fauna of the warmer period which followed was first described from Upton Warren in Worcestershire, and this place has given its name to the complex Mid-Devensian (Weichselian) interstadial of the English Midlands, which is correlated with Continental interstadials of similar date. At Four Ashes and Earith deposits of this warmer period overlie the layers containing the arctic fauna. Radiocarbon dates fall within the period 38,000 to 42,000 years ago. Pollen analysis of the Upton Warren deposit—a series of silt bands within terrace gravels of the Salwarpe, a tributary of the Severn— showed a total absence of thermophilous trees and such great scarcity even of *Pinus* and *Betula* pollen that no local woodland could have been present. But the herbaceous plant species identified from seeds and other macroscopic remains suggested a climate similar to that of south Sweden today, rather than Arctic tundra. The insect assemblage at Upton Warren contained no tundra species, but many relatively thermophilous species now found from south Fennoscandia southwards, and in general indicated an average July temperature of at least 15°C. It is therefore difficult to account for the absence of trees on climatic grounds and an explanation based on delayed migration seems more probable. On the other hand, the fauna of large herbivorous mammals revealed by remains at Upton Warren—mammoth, bison, woolly rhinoceros, reindeer and horse—has suggested a biotic explanation, in that grazing pressure may have been sufficient to prevent colonisation by trees and shrubs of the rich herbaceous vegetation.

The Upton Warren interstadial is now known to have been followed by a tundra period of about 12,000 years which immediately preceded the maximum expansion of Devensian (Weichselian) ice sheets in Britain—the expansion recorded by the presence of Irish Sea till above the interstadial deposits at Four Ashes, and by the Dimlington sequence. The next interstadial known from Britain is of Late-Devensian age and will be discussed in the next chapter. The deposit at Fladbury, from a river terrace of the Avon, which on its radiocarbon date of 38,000 B.P. seemed to fall within the Upton Warren Interstadial complex, has a full-glacial type of fauna of such predominantly arctic beetles that it seems likely that the date is in error, as the sample was collected many years ago and stored in tissue paper.

Devensian (Full-glacial) vegetation

Few deposits of the very cold periods of the glacial stages have proved suitable for preparation of a pollen diagram recording vegetation changes in temporal succession. The "Arctic beds" recovered from terrace deposits of the rivers Cam, Lea and Colne have been recognised as "formed and preserved by temporary and local changes in the valleys, rather than as a result of a general climatic shift" but nevertheless "may provide for us that evidence for which biogeographers have so long sought, evidence of the biota that persisted in southern Britain whilst glaciers were still present in the north and west" (Godwin 1964).

Exceptions suitable for pollen analysis have included the sequence of deposits at Wretton in Norfolk, where deposits of the Wissey valley include organic mud of last glacial age filling a meander cut-off pool. Pollen analyses by Dr West (Sparks & West 1972, Fig. 6.14) have revealed pollen spectra made up of types characteristic of periglacial areas—a numerical preponderance of grasses, sedges and herbs of open ground including high frequencies of *Artemisia*, other Composites, Caryophyllaceae and Cruciferae, together with *Plantago* and *Thalictrum*. Tree pollen is infrequent and is made up largely of *Pinus*, assumed to be transported from a distance. There is still however no continuous record of the changes in British vegetation throughout either of the two major cold phases of the Devensian. In the Netherlands the prevalence, outside the limits of the last glaciation, of deposits entirely barren of plant fossils, has led to the supposition that conditions of "polar desert" prevailed there during the periods of most extreme climate.

The Lea Valley "Arctic beds" which gave a date of 28,000 ± 1500 B.P., and the "Arctic bed" at Barnwell Station Pit, Cambridge which gave a date of 19,500 ± 600 B.P. had been known for many years before the development of radiocarbon dating, and their macroscopic remains were investigated by the palaeobotanists Reid and Chandler as examples of full-glacial floras. Unfortunately neither deposit proved suitable for pollen analysis. Both contained the bones of mammoth and reindeer. The two floras appear very similar; no trees, except for the shrubs juniper, dwarf arctic birch (*Betula nana*) and arctic willows, were present, and the vegetation appears to have been a grass-sedge tundra with many herbaceous species which are now of arctic-alpine distribution, including *Dryas octopetala*, *Saxifraga oppositifolia* and *Thalictrum alpinum*. Several plants recorded are no longer native, including *Papaver alpinum* (later recorded by Miss A. P. Conolly from late-glacial deposits at Whitrigg), *Arenaria biflora* and *Potentilla nivalis*, which are high-alpine plants now, also *Potentilla nivea* which is arctic-alpine and *Ranunculus hyperboreus* which is an arctic species (Godwin 1956). The amelioration of climate at the end of the Weichsel glaciation has therefore led, directly or indirectly, to the extinction from the British flora of several interesting arctic and alpine plants—presumably either by the intolerance of these plants for higher temperatures, or by their inability to compete with more vigorously growing or shading plants which successfully invaded Britain at the end of the glaciation.

The Full-glacial floras now known from between Chelford time and the opening of the Late-Devensian period *c.* 15,000 years ago have been discussed by Bell (1969). She points out that, in addition to those species now absent and those now restricted to montane habitats in Highland Britain—the plants which gave rise to the name "Arctic beds"—there are also many species which are now found as weeds or halophytes (salt-tolerant species) or whose present distribution is as southern or steppe plants. The weed element in Full-glacial floras is explained by the absence of competition from trees and shrubs and by the frequency with which soils must have been kept disturbed by frost movements, leading to open communities. The overlap in Full-glacial floras of species now characteristically northern or southern in their distribution suggests that either the Weichselian Full-glacial climate was different from that of any part of Europe today (reconciling the demands of these respective elements which are today satisfied only in quite distinct habitats) or that the present distribution of these species does not accurately reflect their climatic tolerances. For example, *Helianthemum canum* and *Potentilla fruticosa*, which are southern species in the sense that they do not extend north of the Arctic Circle in Scandinavia, are now, within their range, plants of open and refuge situations (see pp. 107–8) rather than of warm situations. The steppe element in the Full-glacial floras may reflect the definition of steppe as "a continental xerophytic vegetation of herbaceous plants " (Böcher). The general presence of halophytes suggests the possibility that saline conditions were associated with permafrost.

4 The Late-glacial period in Britain

The Upper Pleistocene period. (iii) Late-Devensian (Weichselian) deposits and vegetation

THE late-glacial stage of the Devensian (Weichselian) glacial episode ended at the opening of the post-glacial or Flandrian period, ten thousand years ago. Its beginning, regarded as the change from glacial to less severe conditions, is not precisely defined and indeed would be expected to be a non-synchronous horizon, at least between the glaciated and unglaciated parts of Britain, and probably between south and north. The Dimlington date shows that glacial conditions must have prevailed in north-east England 18,500 years ago, and both flora and insect fauna of the Dimlington Silts agree to indicate the extremely harsh conditions of a glacial environment. By 14,500 years ago, ameliorating conditions in north-west England are recorded in an organic lake mud which was then forming in a kettlehole pond in the southern Lake District—a kettlehole within the drift of the most recent glaciation of north-west England. Pollen spectra from this early organic deposit in Blelham Bog indicate late-glacial conditions, as they include a wider range of pollen types and suggest a richer vegetation than do the records from Full-glacial deposits.

The Allerød Interstadial within the Late-Weichselian sequence of North-west Europe was first recognised in deposits in a Danish tile-works at Allerød, north of Copenhagen. During Late-Weichselian times the swollen Scandinavian ice-sheet retreated from its maximum limits on the north German plain and in central Jutland to a final halt across mid-Sweden, where a great belt of frontal moraines, the Ra moraines, indicate a last cold stage before the rapid retreat which set in about ten thousand years ago. The lowest deposits at Allerød are clays rich in remains of the arctic-alpine plant *Dryas octopetala*, and represent deposition during a cold period soon after the retreat of ice from this area: this period became known as Old *Dryas* time. Above the lower *Dryas* clays at Allerød were organic lake muds containing fruits of tree birches and remains of other plants more warmth-demanding than *Dryas*; these were overlain by an upper *Dryas* clay. This sequence was interpreted as indicative of a late-glacial climatic oscillation resulting in a change from a sparse arctic-alpine vegetation and conditions of soil movement favouring the deposition of clays, to birch woodland on stable soils, and then back to tundra conditions and moving soils. The period of birch woodland, evidence for a temperate interlude, was called Allerød time and the second cold period Younger *Dryas* time. This stratigraphic sequence of two inorganic layers separated by an organic layer was then recognised at a number of other sites in North-west Europe, and pollen analysis at these sites indicated a similar threefold division of the profile into lower and upper zones dominated by herbaceous pollen types, separated by a zone dominated by the pollen of tree birches and containing that of other warmth-demanding species such as *Filipendula ulmaria*. These zones were called I, II and III respectively and interpreted as representative of respectively Older *Dryas* time, Allerød time, and Younger *Dryas* time. Subsequent radiocarbon dating assigned to the zone boundaries the dates shown in Fig. 10; it was assumed that the pollen zone boundaries, which corresponded with the stratigraphic changes, represented synchronous climatic shifts. Allerød time, corresponding with the zone dominated by high percentages of tree birch pollen, lasted from *c.* 12,000 until *c.* 10,800 radiocarbon years ago. Unfortunately the section at Allerød was destroyed by later development and no pollen diagram from this type site has been published.

Later work in Denmark showed that at some sites in Jutland the curve for percentages of tree birch pollen had two peaks—a minor peak being present *below* the major expansion of birch pollen within organic sediment which represented the Allerød oscillation, Zone II. In deposits of a former lake at Bølling in Jutland, the lower peak of birch pollen was found in organic sediment, separated from the overlying Allerød layer by a deposit of mineral sediment within which pollen of herbaceous types predominated. The great Danish botanist Iversen interpreted this sequence as indicative of a minor interstadial, called Bølling, before the major Allerød interstadial, and Late-Weichselian temperature curves based on movements of the birch forest belt in North-west Europe have been published (e.g. West, 1968, Fig. 10.6). The Bølling Interstadial divided Zone I into sub-zones Ia, Ib and Ic, in which Ib represented the milder Bølling time and Ia and Ic times called Oldest and Older *Dryas* respectively. Radiocarbon dates for Bølling time published from sites from West Norway to North Germany all fall within a period of *c.* 500 years in the eleventh millennium B.C., but there is no synchroneity comparable with that found for Allerød time.

The cold period (stadial) which followed the Allerød Interstadial and became known as Younger *Dryas* time clearly corresponded with the final cold episode of the Weichselian which caused a major halt in the retreat of the

Scandinavian ice, so giving rise to the Ra moraines. No organic late-glacial deposits have been found north of these moraines, and estimates of the length of Younger *Dryas* time based on radiocarbon dating agree with estimates based on counts of annual laminations (varves) in Sweden to assign a length of about 500 years to this period. The Younger *Dryas* stadial constitutes a major interruption in the progress of climatic amelioration and vegetational change from Full-glacial conditions to the post-glacial development of temperate forest in northern Europe. No comparable stadial can be recognised in the deposits of the corresponding time in North America.

Although it appeared at first that the sequence of Late-Weichselian deposits in the British Isles resembled the classic succession established in Denmark, as more and more sites have been investigated and more detailed methods of analysis applied it has become apparent that major differences exist. These can most easily be explained as the result of regional differentiation in Late-Weichselian climate and vegetation. It is not difficult to accept such regional differentiation when one considers the differences today between Allerød in East Sjaelland—where in cold winters holly is killed, and where ivy seldom flowers and fruits luxuriantly, though, where man allows it, tall beeches and limes form magnificent high forest—and comparable latitudes in West Scotland, where on wet and windswept coasts which are nevertheless kept warm in winter by a warm sea, blanket bog descends almost to sea level but hollies and ivy flourish like weeds, and in the sheltered gardens of Inverewe many frost-sensitive species can be grown. Such regional differentiation must have existed in earlier periods, but only for the last 15,000 years or so do we have sufficient information to be able to understand it in detail.

Sub-division of Late-Devensian (Weichselian) deposits in Britain

In the British Isles, the first evidence for sub-division of the Late-glacial period in agreement with the succession at Allerød was reported from the Wicklow mountains of Ireland in a classic paper by Jessen and Farrington in 1938. At a site, Ballybetagh, on the northern fringe of the mountains, a shallow valley was found to have on its floor lake muds, rich in remains of the Giant Irish Deer (*Megaceros giganteus*), which was common in this period. These were found to be overlain by a solifluction deposit which had sludged down the valley slopes during a subsequent cold period. Analysis of the deposits showed a vegetation succession comparable with that at Allerød, though here no remains of *Dryas* were found in the inorganic deposits above the lake muds: instead, other plants of open habitats, e.g. *Salix herbacea* were found. In the lake muds were macroscopic remains of *Betula pubescens*, and pollen of *Pinus*, as at Allerød, and stomata which at the time were considered to be those of *Pinus*, proving its presence at the site, but later (when

Iversen had recognised *Juniperus* pollen as abundant in Late-glacial sediments) the possibility that these stomata were also of Juniper was allowed.

The division of the Late-glacial period into three sections was thus firmly established: a pre-Allerød cold phase, or Zone I, then the Allerød cool-temperate oscillation, which became Zone II, and then the post-Allerød climatic recession, the Younger *Dryas* cold period, which became Zone III. Recognition of this threefold division followed at a number of British sites, and a picture of conditions in Britain during the Late-glacial period began to emerge. Though often divisible on stratigraphic grounds into the three zones outlined here, the characteristic Late-glacial vegetation of Northern Europe has a unity best expressed by the term "park-tundra" coined by Iversen. In the colder phases of the Late-glacial, and probably at all times in more northerly latitudes and at higher altitudes, the vegetation was a form of tundra in its lack of trees, and often in the open nature of the communities, so that plants unable to thrive in shade or closed vegetation were common. *Dryas* was one of these plants, so also were the dwarf birch, *Betula nana* (Plate 17), and the arctic willow, *Salix herbacea* (Plate 16). All three of these plants are now thought to be intolerant of temperatures above a certain level (though the exact nature of this effect is perhaps still not clearly understood), so that their presence at sea level fixes certain maxima for the Late-glacial temperature figures. During the milder period of the Allerød oscillation, trees of birch, *Betula pubescens* and *B. pendula*, and poplar (*Populus tremula*), grew in many parts of Britain, either as copses amid the generally herbaceous tundra vegetation, or as what appear from the pollen percentages to have been almost continuous woodlands. Iversen's term "park-tundra" characterises this mixture of open herbaceous communities, with copses of the hardier trees as named above, varying in composition with aspect, soil, and topography as well as with latitude and altitude. In spite of the comparative wealth of data available in Britain, it is still uncertain to what extent the tree birches were able to form woodlands during the colder periods of Zone I and Zone III, and it is still not clear exactly where pine was present in Britain during the Late-glacial, apart from its apparently undoubted presence in the south-east. Figures 12 and 13 show that at Hockham Mere there was an expansion of grass and willow, at the expense of birch, in the colder period represented by Zone III.

Certain plants are particularly characteristic of the Late-glacial vegetation in Britain. One of the first woody plants to become established was undoubtedly the willow, probably several species (it is not yet practicable to identify these on pollen alone). A shrub present at some but not all sites was juniper (which, as Iversen pointed out, can exist in a tundra vegetation as a prostrate form, scarcely flowering, but responds to a rise in temperature by putting out flowering, erect branches and developing into a taller shrub)—also sea buckthorn, *Hippophae rhamnoides*, rowan, *Sorbus cf. aucuparia*, and crowberry, *Empetrum nigrum*, which at certain times appears to have formed extensive heaths as it does today in parts of Jutland. A very characteristic group of Late-glacial plants comprises those now found in open habitats. *Rumex, Artemisia, Armeria, Thalictrum, Campanula, Centaurea, Epilobium, Galium, Jasione, Plantago, Polygonum, Succisa* and *Valeriana* are genera which apparently found favourable conditions wherever and in whichever periods there was no closed birch woodland. The earliest pollen spectra at the base of Zone I often consist predominantly of grasses, sedges and willows, which seem to have been the first colonisers of the bare ground when it became stable after the cessation of severe solifluction movements. Of the plants which by their intolerance of shading demonstrate most clearly the prevalent treelessness of long periods of the British Late-glacial, *Helianthemum*, which is widely found, is one of the best examples. Another facet of Late-glacial ecology must have been the prevalence of soils of comparatively high base-status, since the fresh glacial debris of the glaciated areas had not yet been subject to the leaching effect of millennia of rainfall. Of many plants which seem to have been widely distributed during this period and are now, by contrast, restricted to base-rich soils, the Jacob's Ladder, *Polemonium caeruleum*, is a good example. A further group of plants characteristic of Late-glacial vegetation includes those now known as colonisers of new habitats on mountains—the Fir Clubmoss, *Lycopodium selago* (Plate 21), is widely known from the Late-glacial. *Koenigia islandica* (Plate 24), a very rare plant of the Scottish hills, has been recorded in the Late-glacial flora of several sites in England as well as in Scotland.

Probably the nearest approach to the ecological conditions of the Late-glacial period in Britain is found now on mountains of moderate elevation, where the bedrock is reasonably base-rich and weathers in such a way as to renew the base supply—and where conditions have been such as to preserve the habitat from transformation into closed forest during the Post-glacial climatic optimum, and also from the rigours of grazing by rabbits and sheep during recent centuries. Though it is not possible to find anywhere in the world a replica of conditions and vegetation during the Late-glacial period, certain localities in high latitudes suggest certain features of it, but in Britain the nearest approach to the Late-glacial vegetation is to be found on certain mountain ledges where tall herbs grow without interference from grazing animals, and in plant communities such as those of Upper Teesdale, where geographic factors have combined to preserve the plants of open habitats and base-rich soils from extinction by forest or by man and his grazing animals during the later Post-glacial period. The recent discovery of *Betula nana* in Teesdale, far from its nearest station in the Scottish Highlands, represents an almost certainly lineal descendant of one of the most characteristic plants of the Late-glacial vegetation. This is what is meant by a "relict" species; *B. nana* is similarly found in an isolated station on Lüneburg Heath in West Germany, and at one locality in the French Jura.

Some Late-Devensian (Weichselian) sites in Britain

Figure 11 shows a pollen diagram from a site in East Yorkshire which lies on the Escrick moraine. Dr Bartley interpreted this sequence as corresponding to the classical Danish sequence and distinguished sub-zones 1a, 1b and 1c on the basis of the curve for percentages of trees birch pollen. Within the organic mud of Zone II tree birch pollen formed more than half the total, indicating the local presence of birch woodland. Within the less organic deposits of Zone III, there was an assemblage of pollen types characteristic of open ground and discontinuous plant cover—*Artemisia, Rumex, Thalictrum,* and Caryophyllaceae types—similar to that found in Zone III deposits at continental sites, together with spores of *Lycopodium selago* (Plate 21). As was customary until very recently, Bartley used "zone" as indicative of the deposits representing a period of time, bounded by supposedly synchronous environmental changes, as it had been used by pioneers of pollen analysis in Northwest Europe and embodied in the late- and post-glacial zonations of Jessen and Godwin.

In southern England outside the limits of the last glaciation comparatively few sites of late-glacial deposition are known. An age of *c.* 13,560 radiocarbon years was assigned to peat erratics found in the valley of the Colne in Hertfordshire; these contained an assemblage of pollen types and macroscopic remains characteristic of late-glacial floras, including genera of open habitats, *Artemisia, Plantago* and *Polygonum,* the shrubs *Hippophaë* and *Ephedra,* together with some pollen of *Salix, Pinus* and of *Betula* including *B. nana.* At Hawk's Tor on Bodmin Moor, on a surface of weathered granite, lay freshwater muds and peats containing a typical Allerød flora, overlain by bands of gravelly soil which had clearly moved down hill slopes by solifluction under periglacial conditions; the muds and peats were disturbed by cryoturbation indicative of very low temperatures. In the peat immediately below this frost-disturbed layer, and in the lowest layers of the organic matter, were found remains of plants—*Betula nana, Salix herbacea, Thalictrum alpinum,* and *Subularia aquatica,* all now restricted to localities in northern England or Scotland, or Wales or Ireland, far distant from Cornwall. The tree pollen throughout the organic layer was of *Betula, Pinus* and *Salix* only, and other plants recognised from pollen and spores were those of genera already becoming familiar as part of the Late-glacial flora of North-west Europe, such as *Artemisia, Armeria, Botrychium, Empetrum, Helianthemum, Selaginella* and *Thalictrum.* An interesting discovery in the mud was an anther of *Myriophyllum alterniflorum,* a plant whose pollen has subsequently been very widely recognised as characteristic of the pools which were so abundant on the uneven Late-glacial land surface. Taken as a whole, the plant assemblage of the mud and peat which underlies the solifluction layer at Hawk's Tor is in agreement with the general character of Late-glacial vegetation, and includes at its upper and lower limits, plants whose present distribution lies far to the north of the site.

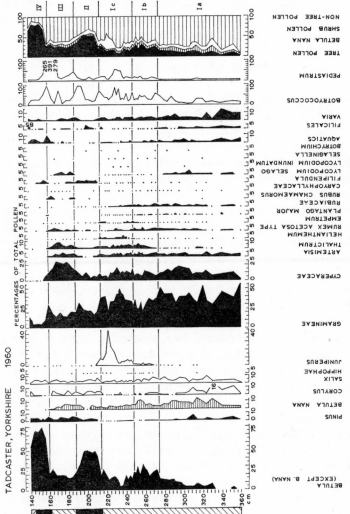

Figure 11. A Late-glacial pollen diagram from Tadcaster, Yorks, after D. D. Bartley. Reproduced by permission of the "New Phytologist" from D. D. Bartley, 61, 1962.

This can be taken as very strong evidence for climatic severity in southern Britain, far outside the limits of recent glaciation, during the Late-glacial period. The physical characteristics of the disturbed gravelly soil which overlies the Late-glacial muds and peats are those which would be expected from a return of a more severe climate involving alternate freezing and thawing, and so leading to typically frost-disturbed soils during Younger *Dryas* time. This is a reasonable amplitude for the post-Allerød climatic recession in the uplands of Cornwall when all evidence is considered.

In North Wales and the Lake District, the presence of corrie moraines had for some time led to speculation about a possible recrudescence of glaciation in the high corries of these mountains, at some time after the retreat of the main Weichsel ice. Evidence on this problem in the Lake District came from cores from the bottom sediments of Windermere, taken in 1938 on the initiative of C. H. Mortimer. They showed an organic mud lying between two layers of varved clay; the lower varved clay was of very considerable thickness and the thickness of each varve increased on passing downwards in the profile, while the upper varved clay was only about 30 cm thick and contained about 400 very narrow varves. The organic layer contained abundant catkin-scales and fruits of *Betula pubescens* and a catkin-scale of *Populus tremula*; also coniferous tracheids which could have been *Pinus* or juniper. Later, pollen analysis of this profile showed that the basal organic mud contained a juniper pollen zone; the overlying birch pollen zone corresponded with the zone of macroscopic remains of tree birches. A date of 11,870 radiocarbon years for the base of the *Betula* zone confirmed that it was of Allerød age, and the juniper zone therefore older. Subsequent work on the nearby Blelham Bog, beneath which is a filled-in kettlehole pond of Late-Weichselian times, confirmed that in this area a juniper-dominated pollen zone within organic mud lies beneath the Allerød birch zone. At Blelham Bog it was possible to get a closely spaced series of eleven Late-Weichselian radiocarbon dates, from which the depth of each annual increment to the deposits could be calculated. By counting pollen grains per unit wet volume of deposit it was then possible to express pollen counts in "absolute" terms—as grains per unit area per year—rather than as percentages. The most striking result of this was to show that there was a tenfold increase in the rate of pollen deposition per year at the lower boundary of the juniper zone. This increase involved nearly all pollen types present and was interpreted as evidence for a major climatic amelioration between 12,500 and 13,000 years ago—that is nearly 1000 years before the opening of Allerød time.

A similarly early date was obtained from organic mud exposed between laminated silts during a dam excavation at Loch Droma in the North-west Highlands of Scotland. This date, of 12,820 radiocarbon years, came from mud containing pollen spectra indicative of several plant communities—those of treeless ericaceous heath, snow patches and wet habitats—and including such interesting records as *Koenigia* and *Saussurea alpina*. The discovery of this deposit showed that no ice had been present in this through valley in the North-west Highlands since a thousand years before Allerød time. Since the publication in 1963 of Kirk & Godwin's paper on Loch Droma, long late-glacial profiles have been described from other lakes of the North-west Highlands including Loch Sionascaig (Plate 6) (Pennington *et al.* 1972) and from the Isle of Skye (H. J. B. Birks 1973).

In Skye and at sites in West Wales the same sequence, of a juniper zone overlain by a birch pollen zone of Allerød age, has been found as in the Lake District. This pattern has not been recorded from continental sites and it is impossible to fit it into the sequence of the threefold division of the classic Danish sequence—Zone I (cold), Zone II (birch zone, mild) and Zone III (cold). If we accept Iversen's explanation of a peak in juniper pollen as the result of a rapid response to ameliorating climate by juniper already present but stunted and sparsely flowering, this pre-Allerød amelioration could represent that called Bølling on the Continent; if so, we must accept that there is no evidence in West Britain for any climatic recession in the lowlands comparable with that represented by Zone Ic in the Danish sequence. It seems possible that within the oceanic climate of western Britain no critical climatic threshold was crossed.

Some extremely interesting evidence about immediately pre-Allerød temperatures in West Britain has come from Dr Coope's recent studies of Late-Devensian Coleoptera. Parallel studies of pollen spectra and beetle assemblages has shown that the most warmth-demanding beetles are found in deposits immediately *below* the layer which on both radiocarbon dates and on its birch-dominated pollen spectra represents the classical Allerød. In profiles where a juniper zone is present it occupies the same position in the time sequence as do the most thermophilous beetle assemblages. This is indeed impossible to reconcile with any conception of an immediately pre-Allerød cold period in West Britain. Dr Coope's interpretation of Late-Devensian environmental history is that at an early stage in the period of time represented by Zone I in conventionally zoned pollen diagrams, there was a very rapid rise in temperature, from harsh Pleniglacial conditions where July averages were less than 10°C to July averages of nearly 17°C—though winters may have remained cold. Beetles responded immediately by rapid northward migration, but vegetation history was complicated not only by slow rates of dispersal but by soil conditions. Newly exposed glacial debris presents a skeletal soil not congenial to any but a restricted group of pioneer plants, and so long as winters remained very cold, soil movements would prevent soil maturation. Pollen assemblages from pre-Allerød time in West Britain show much variation from site to site, not only in the presence or absence of juniper but in percentages of herbaceous types.

Dr Birks has attacked this problem by using the method of pollen zonation based on the conception of the pollen assemblage zone as defined by the American Code of Stratigraphic Nomenclature. Each site is described by use of an individual series of zones, which can then be compared with those from neighbouring sites in a search for regional pollen assemblage zones. The Isle of Skye, on which he worked in detail, presents the great diversity of habitat and local climates found in a mountainous island which includes very different rock formations. At five contrasted sites Dr Birks was able to show a diversity in Late-Weichselian flora and vegetation as great as that shown by the modern vegetation, which he analysed by phytosociological techniques. Before c. 12,250 B.P. herbaceous vegetation prevailed. At all sites there was a consistent increase in pollen frequencies of juniper from c. 12,250 B.P., and in birch from c. 11,800 B.P.; the vegetation changes indicate "progressive stabilisation of the Late-Devensian landscape" (Birks, 1973, p. 382). This sequence, like that from Blelham Bog, shows no evidence for any climatic or vegetation recession during the time which corresponds with the Bölling – Alleröd stade, represented by zone Ic in the Danish sequence. Evidence is found in Skye for post-Allerød climatic deterioration, from c. 10,800 B.P., during the time which corresponds broadly with Younger Dryas, in lithological changes in lake sediments and in pollen spectra dominated by grasses, sedges, and *Betula* cf. *B. nana*.

Dr Coope's work on beetles suggests declining temperatures throughout the classical Allerød period, while birch woodlands occupied most of Britain south of the Highlands but were of restricted distribution in Ireland. Evidence from plants, beetles and sediment composition all agrees to indicate very low temperatures and harsh conditions for much of Britain during the post-Allerød cold period, Younger *Dryas* time (Zone III).

The extent of that recrudescence of glaciation during Younger *Dryas* time which is shown by the post-Allerød varved clays of Windermere is a fascinating problem of geomorphology. The existence of long late-glacial profiles at so many sites in Scotland is evidence for an earlier deglaciation than was for a long time thought likely. It now seems probable that general post-Allerød glaciation (the Loch Lomond Readvance) was confined to the high part of the mainland Western Highlands from Loch Lomond to Loch Maree, with isolated small glaciers on other mountain groups. Apart from some particularly oceanic and sheltered western sites, the general prevalence of pollen of *Artemisia* and other plants of open ground, together with stratigraphic evidence, points to periglacial conditions and almost universally frost-disturbed soils throughout most of Britain.

5 The early Post-glacial period; Britain still part of Europe

Early deposits (transitional from Late-glacial)

MOST profiles which contain the transition from Late-glacial to Post-glacial sediments are the lake muds of the many lakes which occupied hollows in the Late-glacial land surface. The change in vegetation recorded by the pollen percentages is in many of these profiles rather sudden, occupying only a few centimetres of the vertical profile, and this suggests that the rise in temperature which ended the post-Allerød cold phase was a rapid one. The general change which marked the end of late-glacial conditions appears to have involved a rapid rise in average and winter temperatures which ended the processes of solifluction and cryoturbation in the lowlands. This would permit the development of a stable soil surface and the initiation of soil maturation, which in itself would modify the vegetation by allowing the establishment of plants which do not tolerate an unstable soil—a group which includes most forest trees. The rise in temperature would of course directly modify the vegetation by permitting plants to disperse northwards and to higher altitudes where they had previously been unable to survive because of low average or extreme temperatures.

The result of these two effects of rising temperatures was a rapid replacement of prevailingly treeless vegetation, tundra or grassland, by woodland or forest. It seems very probable that tree birches had survived from the Allerød interstadial in particularly sheltered and southern localities, such as Hampshire, and in all English and Welsh pollen diagrams the opening of the Post-glacial period is characterised by a decline in the proportion of pollen of grasses, sedges and other herbs, which had been important contributors to the late-glacial pollen rain. The corresponding increase is in the proportions of first juniper, then birch and pine.

Holmes (1964) working on the sedimentology of deposits of this age in Windermere, concluded that a major difference between the inorganic varved clay of Younger *Dryas* time and the basal post-glacial mud which immediately overlies it was not only the increased proportion of total organic matter in the mud, but the fact that certain humic acids began to enter the lake at this horizon. The clearly visible lithological change between clay and organic mud is very largely due to flocculation of the clay colloids by humic acids, and therefore represents a horizon of major importance in the maturation of soils in the drainage basin of the lake—from skeletal mineral soils of glacial conditions to soils which rapidly accumulated humus under stable post-glacial conditions. As yet comparatively little work has been done to investigate how far this process of soil maturation proceeded during the Allerød Interstadial, but the Allerød soils must have been largely destroyed by the severe frost movements known to have affected even the lowlands of Britain during Younger *Dryas* time.

Though juniper was not present at all sites, a characteristic feature of the change from tundra to forest vegetation was a temporary maximum of juniper pollen, interpreted by Iversen as the immediate response to rising temperatures of plants already present in stunted form. As migration of tree birches from the favourable localities to which they had been restricted during the cold Younger *Dryas* period clearly proceeded rapidly, the juniper stage was short-lived as the shrub was shaded and killed by taller trees. Birch pollen rapidly reached up to 90 per cent of total pollen at sites in England and Wales. At Scaleby Moss in north Cumberland the juniper maximum fell between 10,150 and 9550 years ago. One can imagine the final late-glacial vegetation of much of Britain as a heath of grasses, sedges and crowberry, scattered with juniper and willow bushes, and including many herbaceous plants of which the meadow-sweet, *Filipendula ulmaria*, was very characteristic.

Into this vegetation the numerous light seeds of birch, the pioneer tree, would rapidly disperse and grow up to form a forest of increasing density, with disappearance of juniper. In southern Britain, as at continental sites, pine then spread rapidly into the birch forest. Herbaceous plants probably remained well represented in the vegetation for some time, especially in view of what has been found in North America from absolute counts of the rate of pollen sedimentation per year. As the forest became more closed, however, the herbaceous plants of open ground which require light would everywhere disappear, and the pollen of herbs of the forest floor is seldom found in counts, presumably because this pollen was entirely confined to the lower layers of air in the forest and was not dispersed.

In zoning pollen diagrams over the Late- to Post-glacial transition, the top of the Late-glacial Zone III is placed at the decline of the herbaceous assemblage usually characterised by *Artemisia*. The juniper maximum, where present, has sometimes been placed in a transition Zone III-IV. Zone IV is the birch zone.

Zonation (division) of pollen diagrams

Post-glacial deposits in North-west Europe and the British Isles were zoned on changes in the proportions of pollen contributed by the different forest trees. The zonations of Jessen and Godwin were based on the conception that major changes in forest composition were the result of interaction between the post-glacial migration rates of tree genera and climatic change. The changes in forest composition were therefore supposed to be broadly synchronous within a vegetation region such as the deciduous forest zone of Northern Europe. When the introduction of radiocarbon dating made it possible to test this hypothesis of synchroneity of zone boundaries, it at first appeared that the boundaries were indeed synchronous within this area (Godwin 1960). At about the same time, Professor Mitchell in Ireland began to question the validity of any supposedly synchronous zone boundary within the last 5000 years, because the all-important effects of man on vegetation within this period had become recognised. Controversies about methods of zoning pollen diagrams, outlined in the last chapter, were given new impetus by the results of more detailed radiocarbon dating, which showed (e.g. Hibbert *et al.* 1971) that some zone boundaries hitherto accepted as synchronous across northern Europe were not in fact so. Also a decade of work on profiles from the north of Scotland has shown that there are parts of Britain where it is not possible to use the Godwin system of zones since these are based on expansion of trees of the mixed oak forest, which did not take place there in any part of the Post-glacial. A division of the Post-glacial into Flandrian Zones, FI, II and III, as used for previous interglacials, carries similar limitations.

In these circumstances there is an increasing use by pollen analysts of plant names, rather than numbers, for zone titles. If a single plant taxon is over-whelmingly dominant its name is used; otherwise combinations of character-istic genera describe the zone as a Pollen Assemblage Zone. The Godwin series of numbered zones for profiles such as Hockham Mere (Figs 12 and 13) can be re-described as Pollen Assemblage Zones—see West (1971), Fig. 8.

Problems of early Post-glacial vegetation history

One problem involved in comparison of percentage pollen diagrams covering the earliest Post-glacial time is the absence of juniper from some sites—a similarly irregular distribution of juniper in Late-glacial times has already been noted. Absence of juniper inevitably affects the actual percentages reached by other taxa, particularly important being birch, so making numeri-cal comparisons of pollen spectra from different sites of doubtful value. It may be anticipated that these comparisons will be made easier when absolute pollen diagrams for the early Post-glacial period, comparable with those of

Professor Margaret Davis and others for North American sites, become available.

Another problem is posed for British pollen analysts by profiles from increasingly northerly latitudes in Scotland, where the expansion of birch pollen percentages was delayed for a thousand years after it took place in northern England—compare the date date of *c.* 10,150 ^{14}C years B.P. at Scaleby Moss with *c.* 9000 ^{14}C years B.P. at Loch Maree (H. H. Birks 1972) and at Loch Clair (Pennington *et al.* 1972). These two lochs are both in the same part of Ross and Cromarty. This involves recognition of Post-glacial pollen zones below the lowest deposits dominated by tree pollen, for it must be recalled that the Post-glacial period or Flandrian stage is defined as the last ten thousand years and not on its vegetation.

Division of Post-glacial time

Post-glacial time, the last ten thousand years, was first divided by the Scandinavian botanists Blytt and Sernander, on the basis of plant remains preserved in Scandinavian peat bogs. These provided evidence for changes in both temperature and precipitation. Peat sections are a common sight in bogs which have been cut for fuel, and variation in peat type is obvious. It is generally supposed that highly humified peat with decomposed plant remains

TABLE 1

Blytt and Sernander's division of the Post-glacial

Blytt and Sernander period	*Climate*		*Date of boundary*	
SUB-ATLANTIC	Cold and wet	Oceanic		
			c. 500 B.C.	
SUB-BOREAL	Warm and dry	Continental		
			c. 3000 B.C.	{Climatic {Optimum
ATLANTIC	Warm and wet	Oceanic		
			c. 5500 B.C.	
BOREAL	Warmer than before and dry			
			c. 7600 B.C.	
PRE-BOREAL	Sub-arctic			

indicates slow growth of the bogs and a rather dry bog surface, while fresh unhumified peat consisting of easily recognisable remains of the peat-forming plants indicates a wet bog surface and rapid growth of peat. Bog surfaces therefore provide an index to relative wetness of the climate at the time of formation, and their conditions is fossilised in the accumulating peat. Table 1 shows Blytt and Sernander's climatic periods, with the approximate dates assigned to them by subsequent radiocarbon dating.

Though, as will become apparent, evidence from the British Isles does not always correspond with Blytt and Sernander's climatic scheme for Scandinavia, it will be convenient to use their names for periods of Post-glacial time. In general there is probably less certainty now than at one time about interpreting vegetation evidence in terms of climatic change, but taking into account all the evidence the Post-glacial period is still seen as a time during which conditions ameliorated up to an optimum and have subsequently deteriorated.

The Pre-Boreal period

In the early forest period, in the centuries between about 10,000 B.P. and 9500 B.P. plant migration must have been proceeding very rapidly, as less tolerant species which had been extinguished by the glacial conditions re-entered the country, and dispersed rapidly into these plant communities which were not yet totally closed. This extensive juxtaposition of genera, including many not afterwards found growing near together, formed a very interesting vegetation.

No certain estimate exists of the exact amount by which world sea level was lowered by the eustatic fall during glaciations, and as yet there is no *precise* evidence as to how quickly the world's ice-sheets melted during the Late-glacial period with the restoration of former sea level. Before 10,000 B.P. the Scandinavian ice began its final retreat from the line of the Ra moraines; this position represented perhaps approximately half of the total advance from its position at the beginning of the glaciation to its maximum extension on to the north German plain, at the beginning of the Late-glacial period. In North America, there was probably a greater proportion of the expanded polar ice remaining unmelted at the end of the Late-glacial period. This means that the final restoration of sea-level to its interglacial level was delayed until well into the Post-glacial period. At the time under consideration, about 10,000–9500 B.P., sea level was certainly more than a hundred feet below the present, possibly several hundred. A fall of 400 feet is well within present estimates of the maximum eustatic fall during the last glaciations, and it seems probable that during the centuries under consideration, there was free land communication between Great Britain and Ireland. This would involve a position of sea level perhaps 300 feet lower than at present. Of course there is clear evidence that the bed of the North Sea was dry until much later in the Post-glacial, because peat containing characteristic mid-Post-glacial pollen has been dredged from it. In the present state of lack of precise evidence on sea levels in very early Post-glacial times, argument is still possible as to the route by which certain highly characteristic plants reached their present localities in south-west Ireland. Many of the plants making up the "Lusitanian" element of the Irish flora are intolerant of low temperatures, and it seems highly improbable that such a plant as *Arbutus unedo*, the Strawberry Tree, could have survived the Weichsel glaciation under the necessarily periglacial conditions of Western Ireland. It must, it is now thought, have

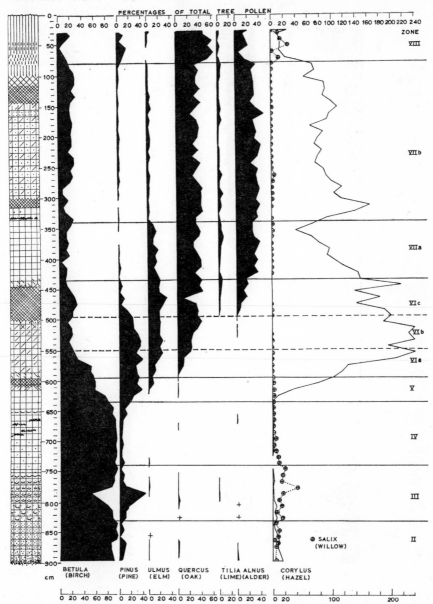

Figure 12. Tree-pollen diagram at Hockham Mere in the north of the Breckland of East Anglia. For comparison with the non-tree pollen diagram (Fig. 13) note especially the 340 cm. level where the strong decline of the *Ulmus* curve indicates the boundary between zones viia and viib. The pollen-zones are fairly characteristic for East Anglia but zone viii is difficult to recognize, especially since *Fagus* is unusually absent. For explanation of symbols in the left-hand (stratigraphic) column, see Fig. 15, page 41, in H. Godwin's "History of the British Flora".

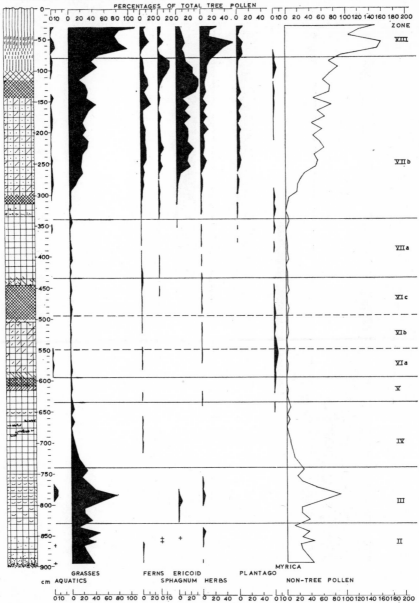

Figure 13. Non-tree pollen diagram at Hockham Mere, Norfolk. In the Late-glacial the ratio of non-tree-to tree pollen is high, but thereafter to the end of zone viia, the very low non-tree pollen values indicate a condition of closed forest cover. Shortly above the 340 cm. horizon, approximately representing the early Neolithic level, the non-tree pollen curves begin substantial and maintained increases which indicate the presence of the great 'heath' communities of the Breckland. Note that pollen of *Plantago lanceolata* (ribwort plantain) corresponds to the general run of non-tree pollen curves. For explanation of the symbols in the left-hand (stratigraphic) column, see Fig. 15, page 41, in H. Godwin's "History of the British Flora".

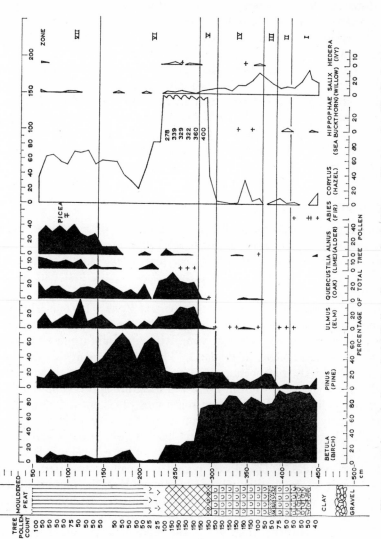

Figure I4. An early Post-glacial Pollen diagram from Flixton, Yorks, after H. Godwin. Figures I2, I3 and I4 are reproduced from "A History of the British Flora", by H. Godwin, by permission of the Cambridge University Press. For explanation of the symbols in the left-hand (stratigraphic) column, see Fig. I5, page 4I, in "History of the British Flora".

survived the glaciation in some south-western refuge, far from conditions of low temperatures and solifluction, and have migrated into Ireland during the early Post-glacial period, along oceanic coastal fringes now submerged. Similar considerations apply to other members of the "Lusitanian" flora of South-west Ireland—i.e. plants requiring highly oceanic conditions and rather high temperatures, which are today found in the western Mediterranean region. As more and more plant records for the Late-glacial flora of Britain accumulate, it becomes increasingly apparent that pollen of plants of southern distribution was indeed present in the rich Late-glacial assemblage, e.g. *Helianthemum canum*, *Ephedra distachya*, and several plants of the family Labiatae. This confirms the possibility of extensive migration of relatively warmth-loving plants into the British Isles, within the period of Late-glacial very low sea level.

The Boreal period

Foremost among the plants not recorded in Britain during Late-glacial times, but apparently early immigrants, are the hazel (*Corylus avellana*), and shortly afterwards, the more warmth-demanding trees, elm (*Ulmus*) and oak (*Quercus*). Hazel pollen reaches very high totals in late Zone V, the first part of the Boreal period, dated at Scaleby at about 9000 B.P., and particularly in the succeeding period, the mid-Boreal, or first part of Zone VI–Zone VIa: see Figs. 12 and 14. The total of hazel pollen grains reaches up to seventeen times the total of other tree pollens at some Irish sites, and up to four times the total of other tree pollens in England. The other trees at this time are mainly pine and birch, pine being more numerous in the south and east, birch in the north and west—but in Zone VIa there are appreciable amounts of elm and oak pollen already present at some sites. It is not therefore quite clear what exactly the forest composition was—the very high values for *Corylus* pollen have suggested a prevalent hazel scrub below a canopy of pine or birch, but the possibility of the existence of pure hazel woods at this time cannot be excluded. The Boreal period is usually considered to have had a less oceanic, more continental type of climate than the present British climate. The pine-woods of the Baltic island of Gotland, with hazel undergrowth, may represent an approximation to the vegetation of South-east England during the Boreal period, but in the more oceanic west more birch remained, and it seems probable that in these regions, in the areas of highest hazel percentages, pure hazel scrub was in places the dominant vegetation.

At the time of the highest values for hazel, in Zone VIa, elm and oak pollen was present at British sites, often in considerable quantity, as in the diagram from north-east Yorkshire in Fig. 14. These two warmth-demanding trees seem to have spread fairly rapidly across the British Isles—from the land bridge with France by which they presumably entered—for they appear at the same horizon in diagrams from southern Scotland and from Western Ireland.

In Iversen's discussion of the role of elm and oak in early Post-glacial forest development, he points out that when climate and soil permit their growth, these trees, being longer-lived, compete successfully with "pioneer" species like birch, and eventually replace them in a climax forest. At sites in southern England the expansion of oak and elm within the period represented by Zone VI was accompanied by steep falls in birch and pine, resembling the continental pattern (Fig. 12). In northern England and Scotland, by contrast, percentages of pine increase at most sites to a maximum in late Zone VI (VIc)—see Figs. 14 and 15. Hibbert *et al.* (1971) dated this pine maximum at Red Moss, Lancashire, to the period between 8000 and 7000 ^{14}C years ago: there is a similar date from Burnmoor Tarn in Cumberland. Three dated profiles from North-West Scotland show that at Lochs Maree, Clair and Sionascaig pine replaced birch or birch-hazel as the dominant tree at a time between these two dates. The late expansion of pine as a forest tree in Highland Britain, and local variations in its distribution shown by, for instance, its virtual absence at Scaleby Moss, suggest that soil conditions played a major part in determining its success. In northern England and southern Scotland the pine phase of Zone VIc was temporary and followed by expansion of oak and alder balanced by steeply falling pine, but in that part of northern Scotland where pine or pine-birch is the native forest type today (McVean & Ratcliffe 1962) no expansion of oak, elm or alder pollen has yet been recorded. The changing composition of British forests at the end of the period represented by Zone VI is an intriguing ecological problem. Interpretation of percentage pollen figures is complicated by the inevitable percentage changes in all taxa brought about by major changes in one or two. It is to be hoped that in time to come, comparison of dated absolute pollen diagrams will give us more understanding of these changes. The role played by the alder in this period before its rapid expansion is not clear, and the decline of pine at many sites would appear to have been followed by growth of deciduous trees in its stead, which poses problems in understanding the succession.

The Boreal-Atlantic transition

At this point it is pertinent to summarise briefly the evidence for climatic change at this time, about 8000 to 7000 years ago. In the gradual extension through the Boreal period of the more warmth-demanding trees, elm and oak, at the expense of the less demanding birch and pine, is seen evidence for a progressive change in climate towards conditions favouring the warmth-demanding (thermophilous) trees, and this conclusion is strengthened by the appearance in Zone VIc in the south of England of the lime (*Tilia*)—the most thermophilous of native British trees: see Fig. 12. The following,

Atlantic period, Zone VIIa, is generally regarded in north-west Europe as the time of most favourable climate—the climatic optimum. It coincides with the maximum northwards extension of the lime in England. The absence of *Tilia* from the native flora of Ireland is in agreement with the late immigration of this warmth-demanding tree, an immigration consequently delayed until after the steadily rising sea level had cut off Ireland from Great Britain. While overall temperatures were apparently rising throughout the Boreal period, there is considerable evidence for rather dry conditions, particularly towards the end of the Boreal. Low lake levels are suggested by the reworking of marginal deposits in many profiles, including Hockham Mere. In several parts of highland Britain, there is evidence for drying out of mire surfaces at this time, followed by restoration of wet conditions at the mire surfaces during Atlantic times, though at many lake sites the evidence is not conclusive. In these Late-Boreal dry conditions, the spread of alder would be necessarily restricted, because though it does occur as a component in hillside woodland, alder is primarily a tree of wet places—swamps and streamsides. Alder pollen is present in many profiles in Zone VI, and its early presence in Irish pollen diagrams is evidence that the immigration and spread of this tree had occurred before Ireland was cut off by the rising sea level. The formerly accepted explanation for the very sudden expansion in the proportion of alder pollen, which occurs at what appears to be a comparable level in British pollen diagrams, was that the increase in oceanicity, which Blytt and Sernander originally used as the diagnosis of the change from Boreal to Atlantic period, resulted in a fairly sudden expansion of habitats open to the alder, by a rise in ground water level creating new swampy land. This explanation must now be considered against the background of recent radiocarbon dates, which have shown that the expansion of the alder, synchronous at between 7100 and 7350 ^{14}C years B.P. at sites in North-west England, was consistently earlier at sites on the Continent and consistently later in North-west Scotland, where at three sites the base of the alder curve comes at *c.* 6500 ^{14}C years B.P. and percentages remain low in comparison with those further south.

This picture of an increase in rainfall at the end of the Boreal period is substantiated by the evidence from Pennine blanket peats originally presented by Dr V. M. Conway. Peat formation on the Pennine plateaux began at the time of the Boreal/Atlantic transition, and became general at altitudes above 1200 feet, where wet alder woods with birch were gradually succeeded by peat-forming communities of *Eriophorum* and *Sphagnum*.

The date of the final separation of Great Britain from the continental mainland has not yet been precisely determined, but available evidence suggests that it took place about the end of the Boreal period. Some climatologists believe that the consequent establishment of a marine circulation around Great Britain would of itself appreciably increase the oceanicity of the climate, in which case it would be expected that hence-forward, the climate of the

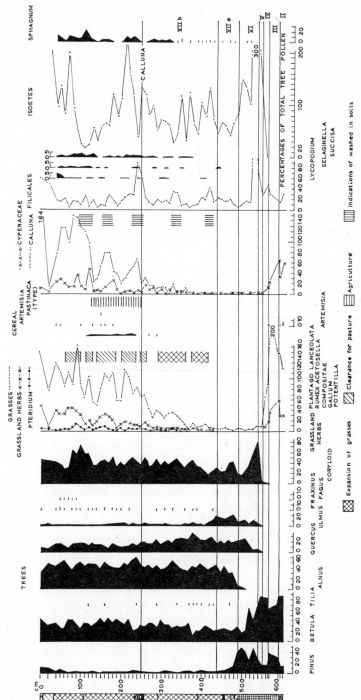

Figure 15. A Pollen diagram from Seathwaite Tarn, North Lancashire. Reproduced by permission of the Royal Society from a paper by the author in *Phil. Trans. Roy. Soc.*, **248**, 1964. The horizon corresponding approximately to 320 cm. has been dated, by radiocarbon, in another core, to *c.* 1080 B.C.

British Isles would be more oceanic than at the same time on the Continent, and that in the Atlantic period, the British climate would be one of extreme oceanicity.

All in all, it appears that the Boreal-Atlantic transition, at about 7500 B.P., is one of the most significant horizons in the history of British vegetation. Not only does it mark what appears to have been one of the most pronounced of the Post-glacial climatic shifts, but it marks the last occasion on which most plants could disperse into Britain by natural processes. The flora at this time represents the true "native flora", and subsequent additions to the flora fall into two categories—a very small group which have a natural dispersal mechanism capable of leaping sea barriers, and a rather large group of plants which, on all available evidence, appear to have been introduced by man, deliberately or accidentally.

The native British flora

The central section of Godwin's book, "History of the British Flora" assembles together all the known facts about the distribution in time of plants now growing in Britain outside gardens and farms. These facts are of course being added to year by year as work proceeds, and new plant records are continuously being made for the deposits of the period so far considered in this book. Because of the necessarily fragmentary nature of the sub-fossil record, the absence of any record of the existence of a plant in Britain since, e.g. the Weichselian glaciation, does not mean that it was not present. The present flora of Britain is known as completely as that of any country in the world, but new records are still being made—i.e. new additions to this flora. Such are the comparatively recent discoveries of *Koenigia islandica*, *Diapensia lapponica* and *Artemisia norvegica* in the Highlands of Scotland. If the data for the present flora of Britain are still conceivably incomplete, how much more so must be our knowledge of the past flora, and so our judgement as to whether a certain plant is, or is not, native, must always be to some extent tentative if dependent on the absence of any sub-fossil record. There are, however, other criteria which can be applied, and one of these is the type of habitat and community in which a plant is found growing. Of the species of elm, for instance, *Ulmus glabra* is the only one now occurring in what appears to be a natural plant community, and it seems reasonable to deduce that it is the only species which entered Britain before the severance from the Continent.

The poverty in species of the British flora, as compared with that of continental Europe, is explicable at least in part as due to the failure of many plants to migrate into Britain by natural dispersal from their southerly refuges before the land connection between Britain and the Continent was severed. When the rapidity with which forest seems to have replaced open vegetation throughout England at the end of the Late-glacial period, is remembered, then it is readily understood how many, particularly the shade-intolerant, of the extinguished herbaceous species may have been so slow in their northward migration as to have failed to reach Britain before it became an island. This seems to be the reason why a plant like *Cirsium oleraceum* flourishes on one side of the Straits of Dover but is absent from similar habitats on the British side.

Early prehistoric man and vegetation

Though it is still generally accepted, as Godwin wrote in 1956, that Palaeolithic and Mesolithic man was dominated by his environment and not equipped to alter the vegetation of forest or tundra, attention has recently been focused on the influence of pre-Neolithic man on British vegetation by Dr Smith, and the important account of Star Carr has been reissued (Clark 1971). At Star Carr a band of Mesolithic hunter-fishers camped beside a now filled-in lake, and made a platform of birch brushwood on top of reedswamp. Pollen analysis of the deposits which soon covered and preserved this Maglemosian site agreed with a radiocarbon date (9500 years ago) to show that the settlement dated from the Pre-Boreal period. Pollen figures showed no change in the proportions contributed by the various trees and no increase in any herbaceous pollens of the kind associated with later human settlement. At Star Carr the settlers clearly lived on a diet of herbivorous mammals with red deer overwhelmingly predominant. Fruits and seeds of weed species including *Urtica dioica* and *Stellaria media* were however found, and the presence of clearings in the forest can be supposed.

It now seems possible both that certain Mesolithic flint axes could have been used for felling trees and that deforestation of some of the heaths of southern England could have originated in the use of fire by early man. Several authors have drawn attention to the rich source of human food provided by the Boreal hazel forests, and it has been suggested that increases in proportions of hazel in pollen diagrams of this period may be the result of man's activities, particularly as hazel is resistant to fire.

At Shippea Hill in Fenland the layer of Mesolithic artifacts falls exactly at the Boreal/Atlantic transition as defined both by date (just after 7600 B.P.) and the rapid expansion of percentage of alder pollen. No certain evidence for any connection between human activity and the decline of *Corylus* and *Pinus* at the end of Boreal times has however been found.

6 *Britain becomes an island; the climatic optimum*

The Atlantic period

WHEN pollen diagrams from southern Britain are compared, there is a remarkable degree of uniformity from site to site in the pollen spectrum of the Atlantic period, Zone VIIa, which·lasted from about 7500 B.P. until about 5000 B.P. Only on the flatter mountain tops above about 1200 feet was the extreme oceanicity of the climate bringing about replacement of deciduous forest by blanket-peat-forming communities. On steep, well-drained mountain slopes deciduous forests extended to altitudes of at least 2500 feet in the English, Welsh and Scottish mountains (as shown by the pollen diagrams from respectively, Red Tarn on Helvellyn, Cwm Idwal, and Lochan nan Cat on Ben Lawers). In Ireland, the forest extended over great lowland areas now covered by blanket peat and raised bogs. There is little evidence for the existence of scrub or grassland at this period, except for the high montane grassland above perhaps 3000 feet. Open habitats must have been restricted to unstable scree, and to the shingle, sand and silt of the sea coasts and estuaries. There were apparently certain areas where local conditions acted against the development of closed forest—such was the "sugar limestone" of Upper Teesdale, where, as has already been pointed out, many plants of open habitats characteristic of the Late-glacial period were able to persist through the subsequent forested periods. Another area which is possibly of this type is the bare limestone pavement of certain areas such as parts of the Burren in County Clare.

The composition of the forest did indeed show some variation from one part of Britain to another. Over most of England, pine had practically disappeared, and the forest consisted of oak, elm, alder and lime, with birch in the north and west, but little in the south and east. (Contrast Figs. 12 and 15.) Unfortunately, it is not as yet possible to separate *Quercus robur* from *Q. petraea* on pollen morphology, and preserved macroscopic remains of the oak are relatively scarce, in this mid-Post-glacial period of high forest. The conditions of soil stability typical of such a vegetation usually lead to complete microbiological breakdown of plant residues, and little or no preservation of recognisable remains. It would seem very likely, however, that the two species of oak were already separated on their ecological preferences, *Quercus robur* dominating the lowland deciduous woods, particularly on heavy clay soils, and *Quercus petraea* occupying the highland zone of the north and west, particularly on siliceous soils. *Ulmus* pollen was certainly that of *Ulmus glabra*; *Alnus glutinosa* is the only British species of that tree. *Tilia cordata*, was, on the pollen record, by far the most common lime in Britain, though *T. platyphyllos* has been recorded in quantity from Norfolk, Cambs. and Warwickshire and occasionally from other parts of England. *T. cordata* did not reach northern England, the apparent limit of its natural expansion, until the opening of Zone VIIa. The scarcity of pine in the English, Irish and Welsh Zone VIIa forests extends into Southern Scotland and the Midland Valley; the strongest contrast in forest composition is between all these areas and the eastern Scottish Highlands, where pine remained an important forest component throughout the Post-glacial period. The Scots Pine of the native Scottish Pine forests of the Highlands is distinguished as var. *scotica* of *Pinus sylvestris*, on the shape of its crown, and on the basis of somewhat shorter needles and cones than the pines now found in England. As yet, there is no means of knowing whether the Boreal pine forests of Britain south of the Highlands were of the Scots sub-species, or of the type now found planted in England (or descended from planted trees). Pine has also been re-introduced into England from Scottish seed.

In general, this Atlantic period corresponds with the period of widest distribution of *Tilia*, the most exacting in its climatic requirements of the forest trees of Great Britain. Certain aquatic plants of "thermophilous" tendencies, notably *Naias flexilis* and *Naias marina*, have been found in the sub-fossil state sufficiently often to give an adequate idea of their distribution, and to show that there has been a contraction in this distribution since the first part of the Atlantic period, which seems to have been the time of maximum temperature—i.e. the Post-glacial climatic optimum. In Scandinavia, the Atlantic period is characterised by the greatest abundance of the ivy (*Hedera*) in Denmark, and the Great Sedge (*Cladium mariscus*) in Sweden. These plants are both sensitive to the low temperatures of continental winters, and their relative abundance in Atlantic times contributed to the diagnosis of this period as one of oceanic climate and optimal conditions in the Post-glacial. In Britain, no decrease in ivy or *Cladium mariscus* occurs at the end of the Atlantic period, and it seems probable that no climatic control of these species has occurred within the amplitude of the post-Atlantic climatic changes in oceanic Britain. It must therefore be realised that the concept of a climatic optimum must differ from one region to another. On the basis of the distribution of the lime, the Atlantic period could be designated as Britain's climatic optimum, but on the basis of general vegetation history, Dr Conway has questioned whether it is appropriate to apply this term to a period which saw the replacement of the Pennine forests above 1200 feet by *Eriophorum-Sphagnum* bogs. Whereas in Denmark's more continental climate, it does seem appropriate to apply the term "climatic optimum" to the period which saw the greatest abundance of a plant of such tropical affinities as the ivy and of the warmth-demanding pond tortoise.

Another striking change in the vegetation of Britain during Atlantic times was the beginning of the development of the raised bogs, or "domed bogs" the great stretches of *Sphagnum* peat which grew up over former lake beds, now filled in by a normal hydrosere, and over coastal flats of impermeable clay, and in parts of the country where the general topography led to flat ill-drained areas, such as the Somerset levels and the Lincolnshire flats round the Humber. In parts of the country, including the estuaries round More-cambe Bay, the Lancashire coast, and places along the Welsh coast, the balance between the eustatic rise in sea level and isostatic movement of the land had been to produce a Late-Boreal to early Atlantic "marine transgression" about the time of the final eustatic rise in sea level. This carried the sea some miles inland, from the present coast, and a bed of marine clay filled the lower valleys and extended over the lower parts of the coastal plain. Later emergence of the land then converted these estuarine clays into freshwater fens, and on top of the fen reedswamp peat, rapid growth of *Sphagnum* proceeded during the oceanic Atlantic period, until the surface of the *Sphagnum* peat rose high above the ground water level, and the peat became ombrogenous. This term means that the peat-forming vegetation is completely separated from ground water or mineral soil, and is dependent on rainwater alone for its supply of necessary mineral salts. The shortage of dissolved bases means that such ombrogenous peat becomes highly acid, and only a very specialised vegetation, consisting mainly of *Sphagnum* species, will grow.

The Atlantic period therefore saw the beginning of that characteristically oceanic and British vegetation type—i.e. ombrogenous peat, in the form of raised bogs where topography favoured this development, and in the form of blanket bog where especially heavy rainfall allowed the growth of ombro-geneous peat even on sloping ground (so that the peat mantled the earth's surface in a "blanket")—this developed on the high Pennine plateau and began to form in parts of Scotland at this time.

Submerged forests

Since the restoration of world interglacial sea level which was apparently completed by early Atlantic times, changes in relative level of land and sea have been brought about by uplift or by downwarping of the land. Britain has, broadly speaking, tended to rise in the north-west and sink in the south-east. The submergence of coastal forests brought about by the sinking of the land relative to the sea has produced the "submerged forests" of many coastal areas, south of the Humber, on both east and west coasts. These submerged forests may be of very different ages, because once the climax of the eustatic rise in sea level was reached, then local rather than general conditions governed submergence.

The Fenland deposits

The Fenland surrounding the Wash constitutes a part of Britain where an especially complex interdigitation of peats and marine sediments has resulted from local changes in sea level. Great tracts of land here lie so near to sea level that the rivers have very little fall, drainage is easily impeded, and a rise in sea level can bring the sea far inland. During the Boreal period, when the Wash and southern North Sea were dry land, formation of fen peat began in the channels of some of the rivers of Fenland, and records a vegetation of forest on the land between the rivers, a forest dominated by pine, with oak, elm and hazel; the small quantities of grass and sedge pollen, and fern spores, presumably record the vegetation of the forest edges and wet drainage channels. Within peaty deposits of this type, at Shippea Hill near Ely, just at the change from Boreal to Atlantic periods, a sandy layer in the peat was found to contain flint flakes of a Mesolithic microlithic industry, subsequently dated by radio-carbon to 7600 B.P. $\pm$ 150. Above this sandy layer is more fen peat, in which the pollen spectrum records a typical Atlantic forest, of oak, lime, elm and much alder, with pine reduced to a very low level. The formation of fen peat became general in Fenland woods as the Atlantic period proceeded, presumably in response to the wetter climate, and the deposits of this period are typically a brushwood peat on the Fenland margins, as at Woodwalton in Hunts, and a fen peat in the true Fens, the lower and wetter lands, as at Shippea Hill. These peats of Boreal and Atlantic age are known as the Lower Peat of Fenland.

Climatic-climax forest

The general Atlantic vegetation of mixed-oak forest or Quercetum mixtum on dry land habitats has been described as the "climatic climax" vegetation of Britain—that is, the final stage of a natural vegetation succession under approximately constant climatic conditions. This mixed-oak forest can be visualised as in places pure oakwood, in places a mosaic of oak, elm and lime (where elm and lime would tend to occupy the better, more base-rich soils), and in places, including most of the north and west, containing much birch. In Ireland and most of Scotland there would be no lime; in the Scottish Highlands pine and pine-birch forests provided the only other type of climax

British forest. Alder would be predominantly the tree of wet places, as in Fenland where it grew in peat-forming communities, but some pollen diagrams from upland country suggest that hill alderwoods were present at this time, in situations which were much later overgrown by blanket peat.

This conception of a continuous forest cover over all the dry land, to altitudes of at least 2500 feet, and bog-forming or fen communities in the wet places, means that the habitats for plants intolerant both of shading and of wet acid conditions would be very much reduced. As we have seen, the only remaining open habitats are likely to have been on the sea coasts and the tops of the highest mountains, apart from certain areas where local topography was unfavourable to tree growth, and which consequently provided "refugia" for many plants which do not tolerate forest or mire conditions, through the mid-Post-glacial forest period. The most important and well-known of these refuges is the sugar-limestone area of Upper Teesdale, where can be found many plants whose ancestors grew together in the rich herbaceous vegetation of the Late-Glacial and pre-Boreal periods (see Chapter 10).

By the time when the Atlantic mixed-oak forest was established, the areas available for plants requiring open habitats must have been very greatly reduced. This is shown by the almost complete absence from the pollen record for Zone VIIa of two genera of exclusively open habitats—*Rumex* and *Artemisia*. Many other interesting plants, incapable of competing with trees in a climate so favourable to trees, must have declined enormously during the forest period compared with their widespread distribution in Late-glacial and Pre-Boreal times. Some of these genera, like *Rumex* and *Artemisia*, returned in strength when, after the Atlantic period, man began to destroy the forest and cultivate the ground; these genera include some of our most characteristic "weeds". Others, including species of *Potentilla*, *Plantago*, and many Composites, became characteristic herbs of anthropogenic grasslands. Still others, such as *Saxifraga* species retreated to mountain refuges. Apart from these mountain and "refuge" habitats, the sea coasts probably provided the situations where most of the herbs, which disappear from the pollen record in the Atlantic period of high forest, survived.

Subsequent modification of the Atlantic forest

In the course of considering the changes which have produced our present British vegetation from this Atlantic forest, it is necessary to know something of the two major factors which have brought about the changes. One is the degree to which the climate has changed since the establishment of the Atlantic mixed-oak forest, and the other is the history of man's effect on vegetation—the so-called anthropogenic factor, which necessitates some acquaintance with modern archaeology. These two factors are sometimes very difficult to separate.

Vegetation changes brought about by natural causes during the second part of an interglacial period, such as that in which we live today, can be studied in the deposits of past interglacials. From these we know that some of the retrogressive changes in vegetation, from that of the middle part of the interglacial, are such as can be attributed to soil changes under the natural process of continued leaching by rain. In the early part of an interglacial, soils of a glaciated area tend to be base-rich, because of the renewal of soil minerals which contain these bases, in the fresh rock-flour ground off the solid rock by ice action and dropped as fresh, unweathered drift. Even in peripheral areas, outside the margin of the enlarged ice-sheets, processes bringing about soil movement under the conditions of low temperatures which accompany a glaciation, tend to renew supplies of unweathered subsoil to the surface soils. In a wet climate, as time goes on, these minerals are decomposed and the soluble bases washed away in drainage water, leaving the soil more acid. This is the process of leaching, and it is of course more rapid in a coarse-textured well-drained sandy soil than in a soil in which drainage is less rapid. Of the forest trees, birch and the conifers are most tolerant of acid soils, as well as of low temperatures. The second half of interglacials is characterised by a return to dominance of these less exacting trees—a phenomenon known as "revertence". Von Post first pointed out that the general course of the curve for birch frequency during the Post-glacial period shows a return to importance in the most recent millennia, which he attributed to revertence. Certainly the Atlantic period of the climatic optimum was the time when birch played a minimal part in the composition of British forests as a whole; at that time it was abundant only in the Highland zone of the north and west. After the Atlantic period, birch tended to return to a more important role in forest composition in general, and this Von Post saw as an index of worsening climate. It also, however, owes something to worsening soil conditions, and during the last thirty years, work on the effect of prehistoric man on vegetation has shown how human interference with virgin forests has always favoured the spread of birch, though this was sometimes only a temporary effect.

Another change attributable to progressive soil leaching is the appearance in quantity of the ling (*Calluna vulgaris*). Andersen found a big increase in *Calluna* in the final stages of the last interglacial, recorded in lake sediments in Jutland. A tendency towards a reduction in mixed-oak forest in favour of *Betula* and *Calluna* could therefore be expected in many places, as the results of progressive soil leaching combined with reduction in temperatures after the period of the climatic optimum. In the second part of our present interglacial, however, man has for the first time become a dominant factor in the ecosystem, and one result of his activities has been to modify the natural vegetation succession in such a way as to favour the spread of *Betula* and *Calluna*. The result is that climatic and anthropogenic factors are intermingled in a most complex manner in the vegetational progression from the climatic climax mixed-oak forest of Atlantic times to our present vegetation, little if any of which can be described as natural. In the next five chapters, a brief account of the known data will be presented.

In those parts of northern Scotland where there is no evidence that climax mixed oak forest ever developed, it seems possible that leaching of soils proceeded so rapidly during the first thousand years of post-glacial time, before the development of birch and pine forests in these northerly latitudes, that edaphic factors controlled the succession. Shallow-rooted heath vegetation does not bring about the recycling of nutrients from deeper layers of the soil on which natural maintenance of soil fertility depends, and in areas of base-poor bedrock in the Northern Highlands it appears probable, on evidence available from lake sediments, that by the time the forest trees arrived much of the country was already too much depleted of soil bases to permit the expansion of the more demanding trees of the deciduous forest. In many parts of Scotland which are treeless today the remains of pine trees entombed in blanket peat show that soil deterioration in this oceanic climate then proceeded further to a point where tree growth was no longer possible. These former forests now buried in peat are found on many Scottish hills at or above the present tree line, as on the hills of northern England and Wales, but in North-West Scotland such buried pine forests are found very near to sea level (Lamb 1964). Pollen analysis has shown that round Loch Maree and Loch Sionascaig there was a very sudden decline in percentages of pine pollen just before 4000 ^{14}C-years ago. More work on ecological history will be necessary before we can know for certain whether the replacement of forest by blanket bog in Highland Britain was wholly the result of the inexorable processes of soil deterioration (see Pearsall 1950, Chap. 9) or whether climatic shifts and the effects of prehistoric land use played a major part in this succession.

7 The Neolithic Revolution; Man begins to destroy the forests

The Sub-Boreal period

THE horizon which ends the Atlantic period, and forms the zone boundary VIIa/VIIb in the British zonation (see Figs. 12, 13, 15), is one of the most interesting and most discussed in the whole history of European vegetation. Originally, Blytt and Sernander defined their Atlantic period as one of oceanic climate in Sweden, separated from the succeeding Sub-Boreal period by an increase in continentality of the climate. This change in climate they found to be expressed in drier conditions in growing bogs, retarding the growth of ombrogenous peat and so represented by a different type of peat from the preceding, Atlantic period. The same horizon was later found to be associated with lower winter temperatures in Scandinavia, for which the evidence was the decline or disappearance of the Great Sedge (*Cladium mariscus*) and the ivy (*Hedera helix*). There is, therefore, good evidence for a climatic change in Scandinavia at the zone boundary VIIa/VIIb, the Atlantic/Sub-Boreal transition. In Britain, however, it has proved impossible to define the opening of the Sub-boreal period by any change in peat type, nor has any clear indication of a change in vegetation likely to have been a direct response to climatic change been found in British pollen diagrams. No significant decline in *Cladium* or *Hedera* pollen occurs. Therefore it seems that within the framework of the more oceanic climate of Britain (compared with Scandinavia) no critical threshold of temperature was crossed by whatever was the climatic change separating the Atlantic from the Sub-boreal.

The Elm decline

Godwin drew this boundary, zone VIIa/VIIb, at the horizon where the curve for *Ulmus*, the elm, shows a steep fall. This horizon can be clearly seen in the pollen diagram from Hockham Mere, Figs. 12 and 13, reproduced from

Godwin's book (1956). This fall in *Ulmus* pollen, the Elm Decline, appears in all pollen diagrams from north-western Europe, and the very considerable number of radiocarbon datings which has been done for this interesting horizon has shown it to be approximately synchronous, within a century or two on either side of 5000 B.P. In spite of at least twenty years of intensive research, no single and universally satisfying explanation of the fall in the elm curve and the accompanying vegetation changes has emerged. The accompanying vegetation changes differ, both within the same country and from country to country, in North-west Europe, but the universal feature is the steep fall in the curve for elm pollen—that is, a sudden diminution in the proportion of the total pollen rain contributed by the elm.

The species of elm involved must differ from one country to another; in northern England and Scotland it must be *Ulmus glabra*, whereas in Denmark there is evidence for the for the presence of other species, and Iversen has postulated that the more thermophilous species *U. minor (carpinifolia)* may have been present in Denmark before the elm decline. In Denmark, the accompanying vegetation changes indicated a possible fall in temperature, as they include a decline in frost-sensitive species—notably in ivy and mistletoe; the decline in ivy has already been cited as evidence for increased continentality of the climate in Scandinavia at this horizon. For Britain as a whole, there is no clear evidence for decline in any frost-sensitive species at the elm decline.

Considering other possible factors suddenly unfavourable to the elm, Godwin has pointed out that though *Ulmus glabra* requires base-rich mull soils for regeneration, the ash, *Fraxinus excelsior*, which at most British sites appears for the first time as a contributor to the pollen rain at the elm decline, is an equally demanding tree as regards soil, so he considers it unlikely that progressive soil deterioration was the cause of the decrease in elm. In spite of widespread conviction among workers in this field that a vegetational phenomenon as ubiquitous and striking as the elm decline must have at least an indirect, if not a direct, relation to a climatic factor, no investigator has been able to produce incontrovertible evidence as to the nature of such a change.

The alternative explanation for the phenomena of the elm decline was originally suggested by Faegri and Nordhagen in Norway, and has been developed in Denmark by the archaeologist Troels-Smith. It rests on the observations of these three authorities that primitive peoples in several parts of the world today use elm leaves as fodder for cattle which are kept stalled, instead of being allowed to graze. This practice is known today in remote parts of Europe, the Caucasus, and parts of the Himalaya, and references to the use of leaves for fodder can be found in British literature down to the nineteenth century. Troels-Smith pointed out that when the first farmers, those Neolithic people who introduced the technique of stock-keeping arrived in northern Europe, the land was covered by "continuous primaeval forest with hardly any grass vegetation" and that no pastures large enough to leave traces of their existence in a pollen diagram were in existence. Therefore the only food for the domestic animals, sheep and cattle, which these people are known to have possessed, was the foliage of forest trees. Elm and ash are the trees whose leaves are most nutritious for this purpose, and before the elm decline, ash seems to have been rare. Ivy is a plant also known to have been used for feeding stock. Troels-Smith in 1960 postulated what is called the anthropogenic explanation of the elm decline; that a new technique of keeping stalled domestic animals was introduced into Europe on a very wide scale at the opening of the Neolithic period, and that these animals were fed by repeated gathering of leafy branches of those trees known to be nutritious— the elms—and by ivy where that plant grew. This would reduce very greatly the pollen production of the elms.

Hibbert *et al.* (1971) have recently shown that a continuous accumulation of radiocarbon dates for the Elm Decline has only confirmed the synchroneity of this horizon at *c.* 5000 B.P. across northern Europe. They use it as the boundary between Flandrian Zones II and III. Studies of both lake sediments and blanket peats have suggested a disturbance of the ecological equilibrium of the preceding period at the time of the Elm Decline. But it is not clear whether the increased rate of soil erosion and accelerated formation of blanket peat indicated by evidence from Highland Britain indicate climatic change alone, and if so precisely what kind of climatic change, or a combination of climatic change and human influence, upon an ecosystem already in precarious balance through soil leaching.

Confirmation of the supposed causal connection between human settlement and the elm decline has come from detailed pollen analysis of the horizon— that is, by counting very large numbers of pollen grains in very closely spaced samples. In Denmark, where this technique was first used, it was found that the first appearance of pollen of the Ribwort Plantain (*Plantago lanceolata*) always coincided with the fall in the elm curve, confirming the association with man. Though there are a few records of pollen of this plant from Late-glacial deposits in Denmark, its spread has been very closely associated with human settlement, which is readily understood in view of its present close association with pastures and waysides. Since the pioneer work of Troels-Smith and Iversen in Denmark, detailed pollen analysis of the elm decline horizon has shown the constant association with it of *Plantago lanceolata* and other plants associated with man, including the nettle (*Urtica dioica*), in other areas of known early Neolithic settlement. In Ireland, the work of Mitchell, Smith, Watts and Morrison has established a close association between the elm decline and such "cultural pollens", in areas for which many radiocarbon dates now prove considerable early Neolithic activity by 5000 B.P. Mitchell believes that the elm decline in Ireland marks the beginning of Neolithic farming, and that as soon as cultivation began, the diminution in elm pollen which had been initiated by pollarding of the trees for their leaves, was continued by the selective destruction of elm trees, which were observed to be growing on the better soils. In the English Lake District, it has been possible to show that the type of vegetational change associated with the fall in the elm curve varies from site to site, and that the cultural pollens are present at this horizon in the areas where there is known to have been a Neolithic population. It seems certain now that, as Godwin had originally suggested many years go, Neolithic activity must have been associated with the elm decline at Hockham Mere, which is close to the great centre of flint-mining at Grimes Graves. At Shippea Hill in the Fens, the elm decline coincides with a Neolithic layer in the fen peat, containing charcoal, flints and bones; from the peat of this layer the dates of 3505 B.C. $\pm$ 120 and 3335 B.C. $\pm$ 120 have been obtained (in radiocarbon years).

Whatever may ultimately prove to have been the climatic character of the centuries on either side of 3000 B.C., the very regular association between the elm decline and the presence of *Plantago lanceolata* is strong evidence that man's activities played some part in the vegetational changes; at the same time, as Godwin has wisely pointed out, it may well be that the great movement of peoples which clearly took place during these centuries, and has left its mark so clearly in the vegetational changes, was itself the result of some far-reaching climatic change which as yet is not fully understood. It has been suggested that the disaster to the elms could possibly have been an epidemic of some parasite of a virulence comparable with the Dutch Elm Disease; this is a theory difficult to prove or disprove, but the more the evidence connecting the elm decline with Neolithic farming and changes in other species accumulates, the less likely does the disease hypothesis become.

Man and vegetation

Palaeolithic and Mesolithic man had comparatively little effect on their environment. The interesting association in the Hoxnian interglacial deposits of a temporary decline in all forest trees with artifacts belonging to a Palaeolithic culture has been mentioned in Chapter 2, but there is no evidence to attribute this episode to man. The characteristic Palaeolithic hand-axe was apparently either a weapon or a grubbing tool, and not until the development of the polished stone axe was man equipped to attack the forests, though forest fires may have been started deliberately. The technological revolution at the opening of Neolithic stock-keeping and agriculture included the development of axes which were made to cut down trees, and this marks the emergence of man as the potentially dominant factor in the ecosystem. If the elm decline is rightly interpreted as the result of the very rapid spread of this new technology through northern Europe, then this horizon marks the end of purely natural forest in this great area. The settlements of people who practised the technique of keeping stalled cattle which were fed on leafy branches, mainly of elm, have been excavated in Switzerland, and the remains of hoards of leaves found in buildings thought to have been stables. This was a definite type of farming culture, considered to have been the earliest of the Neolithic

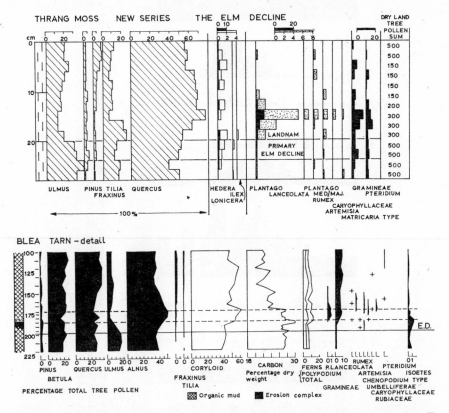

Figure 16. The Elm Decline in North-west England. (i) Thrang Moss, after F. Oldfield. Reproduced by permission from *Geografiska Annaler*, **XLV**, 1963. (ii) Blea Tarn, Langdale. Reproduced by permission of the Royal Society from a paper by the author, in *Proc. Roy. Soc.*, **B161**, 1965.

The date of the horizon E.D. at Blea Tarn is 3150 B.C. ± 120.

in Switzerland and Denmark. As yet, no archaeological remains of such a culture have been found in Great Britain, but it is still possible that it was people of this or a similar culture who were responsible for the *initial* decline in elm. Oldfield, in Lowland Lonsdale (the area around Morecambe Bay), distinguishes in pollen diagrams a "primary elm decline" which may be the result of an initial, and distinct, type of land use, by such a culture: see Fig. 16(i).

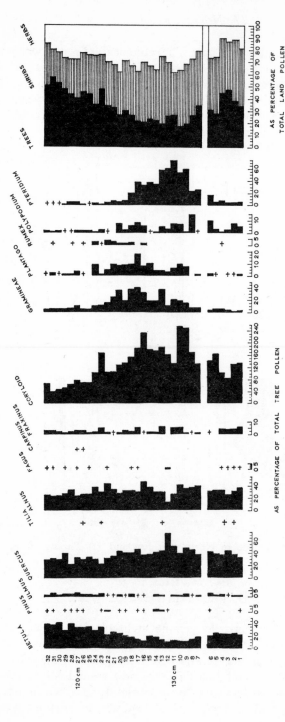

Figure 17. A "small temporary clearance" in the pollen diagram from Tregaron Bog, after J. Turner. Reproduced by permission of the Royal Society from Judith Turner, in *Proc. Roy. Soc.*, **B161**, 1965. This section of the profile formed between 700 B.C. (170 cm) and 400 B.C. (82 cm), and by calculation of average rates of peat formation it can be shown that the three successive phases, of clearance, occupation, and forest regeneration, "could not have lasted much more than about 50 years". J. Turner, 1964, 1965.

DATE	Generalised Raised Bog profile	Tregaron Bog	Various sites	
				SUB-ATLANTIC
1500		Arable Farming Began c. 1182 A.D.		
1000		Celtic Pastoral Farming		
			436 A.D. Retardation layer at Helsington Moss	
500	Fresh Unhumified SPHAGNUM PEAT with *S. imbricatum*	473 A.D. Peat growing at rate 1 cm. in 50 years	Retardation Layers (Minor recurrence surfaces) in the Sub-Atlantic Peat	
	Regeneration Complex	Celtic Pastoral Farming		
A.D. 0 B.C.		404 B.C. Extensive Clearance	450 B.C.	
	MAIN RECURRENCE SURFACE, = GRENZ Dark Humified PEAT (Retardation Layer)	Peat growing at rate 1 cm. in 3 years	to	Late Bronze-Age
500		696 B.C. Fresh peat above Grenz		
		Small Temporary Clearances	900 B.C. trackways	
1000		1004 B.C. Humified peat below Grenz		SUB-BOREAL

Figure 18. A diagram of the Sub-Boreal/Sub-Atlantic transition—the Grenz horizon.

Landnam clearances

In 1941, while the elm decline was still generally attributed to climatic change, and before the power of prehistoric man to dominate his environment had been realised, Iversen published a classic paper attributing certain vegetation changes found just *above* the elm decline to deliberate forest clearance by Neolithic agriculturalists. The pollen curves suggested a clearance of all trees in a limited area, by felling and burning (revealed by a charcoal layer), followed by a primitive form of cultivation of cereals in the cleared patches. Regeneration of the forest followed quite quickly, with colonisation by pioneer trees succeeded by re-establishment of the high forest, in its original form. Iversen attributed this vegetation succession to shifting cultivation by nomadic farmers who moved on to fell a new patch when the first fertility of the cleared ground was exhausted. This, which Iversen called a "Landnam" clearance, differed from the elm decline in that at the clearance level *all* the forest trees were affected—that is, the absolute quantity of tree pollen relative to that of other plants was very much diminished. Iversen interpreted this as wholesale clearance of a patch of mixed forest. The pollens which showed an increase in percentage of the total were grasses, and weeds such as *Plantago lanceolata*, *Rumex*, *Artemisia* and members of the Chenopodiaceae, and then bracken. At the same time, pollen of the cultivated cereals appeared for the first time. Then regeneration of the forest proceeded quite quickly, with colonisation first by birch and other pioneer trees, which were succeeded by oak and lime, and some elm—the trees of the high forest. No selective exploitation of any one tree is involved, and the succession of pollens gives a very vivid picture of the felling, the primitive cultivation, and the invasion of weeds and bracken, and then the stages of return to the original forest. This is a typical Landnam.

At that time (1941) many workers were reluctant to admit that the necessarily small numbers of prehistoric people could have such a profound effect on the local pollen rain, and efforts were made by some to interpret these changes in Sub-boreal pollen curves as due to some climatic change of small amplitude. In 1953, the Copenhagen pollen-analysts carried out a field experiment to demonstrate that it was possible for a small group of men, equipped only with Neolithic axes, to cut down mature trees and clear by burning a fair-sized patch of established forest, within about a week. Polished stone axes from the Copenhagen National Museum were fitted with new wooden hafts, made on the model of those which have been preserved in peat bogs from Neolithic times, and it was found that using these, three men could clear about 600 square yards of forest in four hours. Illustrations of this field experiment, which was carried out at Draved Forest in South Jutland, can be found in Professor Ovington's book on Woodlands in this series. There will be found also photographs of the crop of *Triticum dioccum* (the Emmer wheat which is known to have been cultivated throughout the prehistoric period) which was raised in the woodland soil plus the ashes of the burning, in the year of the clearance (1953) contrasted with the poor crop of the same plant obtained three years after the clearing and burning, when declining soil fertility clearly made it no longer profitable to try to grow cereals there. This doubtless explains the apparent short duration of the Landnam episodes.

This experiment, and the widespread discovery of similar Landnam episodes in many places where the necessarily very closely spaced sampling was carried out, convinced botanists that the Neolithic agriculturalists (not necessarily, indeed almost certainly not, the same cultures as those responsible for the elm decline) were able to destroy, at least temporarily, very considerable areas of primary forest. The polished stone axes of the type used in the Draved experiment were made of flint, and this was apparently a favoured material when available. In those parts of Britain where no flint was available, certain types of igneous rock were found to have the same hardness and response to flaking and grinding. The distribution of these axes, as shown by recorded finds, reveals that there must have been a very considerable trade in them, and suggests the extensiveness of forest destruction which must have resulted from their use. Figure 19 shows a clearance episode recorded in a coastal organic layer in Cumberland, from which a struck flake of flint was recovered, near the site of a microlithic industry.

Sub-Boreal vegetation in Britain—regional differences

When British pollen diagrams for the early part of the Sub-boreal (Zone VIIb) are considered as a whole, it seems likely that the effects of the successive Neolithic cultures, all possibly, at least in part, nomadic, some pastoral and some cultivating primitive cereals in temporary forest clearings, must have altered the composition of the primary forest over most, if not all, of the British Isles, with the possible exception of parts of Scotland, where there is not enough data, as yet, to be sure. The initial disaster to the elm at the elm decline was followed, in some areas, by more or less regeneration of this tree to something approaching its former position as a contributor to the total tree pollen. On poorer soils, likely to have been already impoverished by leaching, elm never regained its status, and presumably was never again an important tree in the regenerated forests. On calcareous soils, as in central Ireland and on the limestone round Morecambe Bay, the percentage of elm pollen was restored after Neolithic forest clearances to something near its former level.

In some areas the effects of Neolithic clearances were more nearly permanent. At the same time as Iversen was, in Denmark, developing the concept of the Landnam, Godwin in Britain was perceiving how the pollen diagram from Hockham Mere suggested progressive deforestation from the horizon of the elm decline onwards, and realising that in this lay the clue to the origin of the Breckland, that great stretch of treeless heath which had

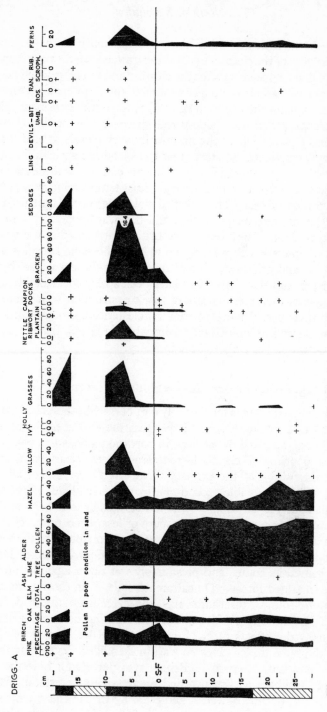

Figure 19. A pollen diagram from Drigg, Cumberland. Reproduced by permission of the Cumberland and Westmorland Antiquarian and Archaeological Society. From Transactions, LXV, N.S., 1965. A struck flake of flint was found at level S.F. In the left-hand (stratigraphic) column, diagonal shading represents sand, and black sections represent peaty humus of buried soils.

exercised the minds of ecologists for many years. To quote Godwin "The deep muds of Hockham Mere provided a continuous picture of the Breckland vegetation from Late-glacial until post-Tudor times, and it was immediately apparent that throughout Zones V, VI and VIIa complete woodland cover must have obtained: throughout this time the total non-arboreal pollen remained a very small fraction of the total tree pollen. Not far, however, above the VIIa/VIIb boundary, the ratio of non-tree pollen to tree pollen rose to high values. From this time forward, grass pollen, ericoid pollen (chiefly *Calluna*), fern spores, *Plantago lanceolata*, and miscellaneous herbs including *Rumex* and many types of Compositae contributed largely to the pollen spectra. When we recall that the Breckland was as densely occupied in Neolithic times as any part of Britain, and that the great flint mines of Grimes Graves lie not far from Hockham Mere, it becomes impossible not to recognise the origin of the present heath communities of Breckland in the forest clearances initated here, as in Denmark, by the Neolithic agriculturalists. The pollen curves appear to indicate that the heaths, once established, remained open, thereafter probably extending, as in Denmark again, during the Iron Age". See Figs. 12 and 13.

Another part of Britain where Neolithic clearances led to what appears to have been more-or-less permanent deforestation was on the coastal plain of south-west Cumberland, a fertile strip of drift-covered lowland between the Lakeland mountains and the sea. In the kettle-holed surface of the drift are many small depressions, some of which contain tarns, and others are now fens or *Sphagnum* bogs. Ehenside Tarn which is a rather shallow tarn which was partially drained in the nineteenth century, is one of the few settlement sites of Neolithic age known in north-west England. The draining of the tarn revealed hearths, pottery, artifacts of wood and bone, a saucer quern, and polished and unpolished stone axes which have comparatively recently been petrologically identified as of Great Langdale origin and Cumbrian type. The outcrops of a particular hard tuff in the Borrowdale volcanic rocks, high on Langdale Pikes and on Scafell and Scafell Pike, were extensively worked to produce these tools. No complete polished axes have been found at the factory sites, but only rough-outs and flakes, so it has been supposed that the rough-outs were finished at lowland settlement sites such as Ehenside Tarn, where sandstone grinding slabs and rubbers were found. Pollen diagrams from the deep muds of Ehenside Tarn, and from three other sites on the coastal strip—Mockerkin Tarn, north of Ehenside, Barfield Tarn, at the southern extremity, and on the sand-dunes at Eskmeals—all agree in indicating a reduction in tree pollen, beginning at the Elm Decline, which seems to indicate a progressive and permanent change in vegetation, from oak woods with elm and birch, with alder and willow in the wet hollows, to progressively increasing grassland with considerable expansion of bracken. Obviously the local history has varied somewhat from place to place, but though local regeneration of woodland may have occurred here and there, the degree of Neolithic activity was sufficiently great to ensure that considerable areas of grass, heath and bracken remained open thereafter, just as in the Breckland; (Walker 1966, Pennington 1970).

The pollen diagram from Eskmeals, which came from an exposed peat band in the side of a newly-dug ditch, where a very fine rough-out of a Cumbrian axe was found in the thrown-out material, shows two successive clearance episodes, which it is possible to interpret as showing a similar history to that of this period in Denmark. At the level of the steep fall in elm pollen, grains of *Plantago lanceolata* and an expansion of grass pollen could agree with the pollarding of elms and simultaneous formation of small settlement clearings; a little above this comes a much more severe clearance episode with not only much greater expansion of grass and grassland herbs, but also the appearance of grains of cereal pollen and of types such as Compositae which are often found as agricultural weeds. This material is so permeated with the roots of modern plants that it is impossible to date, but it would seem that this episode of cultivation may have lasted longer than a typical Landnam.

In Lowland Lonsdale, the south-eastern fringe of the Lake District, round Morecambe Bay, Oldfield has demonstrated a comparable sequence of a "Primary Elm Decline" which is followed by a Landnam episode (see Fig. 16), but the subsequent vegetation history of this area involves more regeneration of woodland between clearance episodes, as if it had been the scene of shifting nomadic settlement, rather than of a denser and more continuous occupation as on the south-west Cumberland coastal plain.

Changes in forest composition resulting from Neolithic activities

The main change in forest composition brought about by these episodes at the opening of Zone VIIb is the appearance of pollen of *Fraxinus*, the ash. At some sites in Britain this tree was present in Zone VIIa, but its main expansion, and first appearance in most parts of the north and west, coincides with the impact of Neolithic disturbance or of temporary clearance of primeval forest. Ash is a pioneer tree in ecological successions, like the birch, and rather light-demanding, so it is possible that though present, it was not able to penetrate into already established oak-elm-birch forest (after its rather later immigration) until the activities of Neolithic man had opened up the forests. In Ireland, ash seems to have been an important forest tree since about 4400 B.P.

It appears that over much of Wales, northern England and southern Scotland and possibly in other parts of Britain too, the Sub-boreal secondary forest, replacing the primary Atlantic forest, was of oak–ash–birchwoods, with alder, and comparatively little remaining elm except in calcareous districts. The behaviour of *Tilia*, the lime, which was at one time thought to have declined throughout the Sub-boreal period under the climatic control of temperatures decreasing from the climatic optimum, has now been shown by Turner to have depended primarily upon the anthropogenic factor. Like the elm, the lime was of use to prehistoric man in a variety of ways, its bast being useful, as well as its leaves nutritious, and furthermore tended to grow on the better soils. Selective felling of lime was therefore very likely, and the final disappearance of the pollen of this tree at many sites has been shown to relate to an episode of human settlement, and to have taken place at different dates in different places.

Those remaining examples of British woodland which show least evidence of disturbance probably approach in composition the Sub-boreal secondary forest. Examples can be found in remaining patches of *Quercus robur* forest, on Midland clay soils, and in the sessile oak-woods with ash, birch and alder in the hills of Wales and northern England, in the Pennine ash-oak woods with elm, and perhaps most striking of all, the high-level oakwoods of Dartmoor and the Lake District, which are discussed more fully in Chapter 10. As yet there is not sufficient data to estimate how much Neolithic man affected the pine and birch forests of the Scottish Highlands. Some of Donner's diagrams from the eastern Grampians suggest that at least some of the clearance phenomena which have been described in this chapter began to appear in Scotland soon after the Elm Decline, but as yet it is not at all clear whether Neolithic man was active in the ancient Scottish pine forests. In the northwest of Scotland, where remains of Neolithic settlement are abundant, in the form of chambered cairns, and settlement sites, such as Skara Brae in Orkney, it is probable, though not yet demonstrated convincingly, that the complete deforestation of much of this area began with such Neolithic exploitation.

Vegetation changes in the Bronze Age

The Bronze Age is now considered to have begun in Britain by about 1700 B.C., but the use of metal tools must have been delayed much later than this in many parts. The detailed work of Turner in Cardiganshire, Somerset, Shropshire and East Yorkshire and in Ayrshire has shown that in many parts of Britain, land use probably altered little, because over most of the highland zone, north and west of the Humber-Severn line, the prevalent pattern of what Turner calls "small temporary clearances" of the Landnam type continued until at least the opening of the Iron Age: see Fig. 20. Doubtless there were exceptions to this; perhaps in other "cornland" enclaves like the Cumberland coastal strip, more-or-less permanent deforestation had set in. Simmonds' work on Dartmoor has shown that the deforestation of that region began during the Bronze Age, in those parts still rich in Bronze Age remains, and there is similar evidence from the Lake District. Dimbleby has been able to show that in north-east Yorkshire, deforestation begun during the Bronze Age initiated the development of podsolised soils with heath vegetation, in areas which had until then been forest. Trying to integrate all these findings into a general picture, it seems possible that whereas in the lowlands surrounding the raised bogs on which Dr Turner has worked, the Sub-boreal forest of the Bronze Age was able to regenerate freely as soon as pastoral

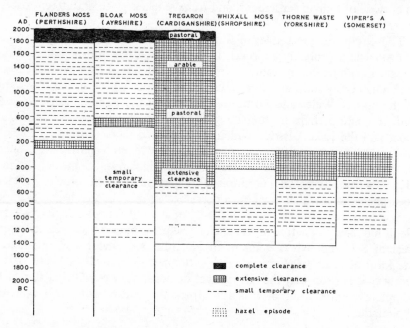

Figure 20. A composite diagram of Bronze Age and Iron Age vegetation history, after J. Turner. Reproduced by permission of the Royal Society from Judith Turner, in *Proc. Roy. Soc.*, **B161**, 1965. The dates are based on radiocarbon evidence.

activities were relaxed in the neighbourhood, by contrast, on light soils (and still more in the uplands) irreversible soil changes accompanied clearances and tended to make the deforestation more permanent.

Of Bronze Age farming on the great area of settlement on the chalk of central southern England, the record in pollen analyses is fragmentary, because of lack of sites of lakes or accumulating peat. From archaeological sources, we know that farmers in this area cultivated the uplands, grew much barley, and became sufficiently wealthy by the 16th century B.C. to support a warrior aristocracy who probably erected the sarson trilithons at Stonehenge. It seems very probable that during the Bronze Age the chalk areas were very extensively cleared of forest, which was probably always rather light, and that

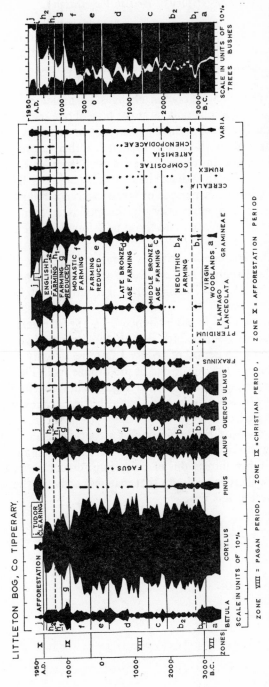

Figure 21. Irish Vegetation History; a pollen diagram from Littleton Bog, Co Tipperary, after G. F. Mitchell. Reproduced by permission of the Royal Society of Antiquaries of Ireland, from G. F. Mitchell, in *Journ. Roy. Soc. Ant. Ireland,* **95,** 1965.

their present vegetation is therefore secondary, resulting from new colonisation by trees, shrubs and herbaceous plants when farming activities were, at
least partially, abandoned, at the end of the Roman period.

Godwin (1962) has described two sites from Kent where pollen preserved
in organic muds recorded vegetation changes beginning *c.* 3650 years ago.
The dominance of herbaceous pollens at the base of one section shows that by
the beginning of the Bronze Age there had already been extensive deforestation
of the chalk country of south-eastern England. Other records of the Bronze
Age vegetation history of this region have emerged from Dr Kerney's work on
the molluscs associated with artifacts in successive horizons from soil profiles
on the chalk. A sequence of periods of forest clearance followed by regeneration can be deduced from alternations in the molluscan fauna between those
now characteristic of woodlands and those now found in open grasslands. A
pollen diagram from Godwin (1962) reproduced in Dr Turner's essay on
"Post-Neolithic disturbance of British vegetation" (in Edit. Walker & West
1970) shows that at Frogholt in Kent there was a great increase in pollen of
plants indicative of forest clearance and agriculture just before 680 B.C.
(^{14}C years).

In Ireland, Mitchell has found evidence (Fig. 21) for extended agriculture
with larger clearances than before, during the Bronze Age, but this was
apparently followed by a period of reduced farming activity and consequent
regeneration of elm and ash, at the end of the Bronze Age. The archaeological
record from Ireland suggests that Bronze Age dwellings were of a temporary
character, probably in woodlands, and that a shifting economy based mainly
on cattle was practised.

In North-west Scotland the beginning of a continuous curve for *Plantago
lanceolata* has now been dated to the years between 1500 and 1800 B.C. at
several sites, and other indications of deliberate forest clearance are present
at some of these, so there is no doubt that man was active in the area of native
pine and birch forest at this time.

8   *Climatic deterioration*

The boundary between Sub-Boreal and Sub-Atlantic periods

THE Bronze Age coincides with the second part of the Sub-Boreal period, a time when on the European mainland it is possible to show that the climate was warmer and drier than at present. Though, as explained earlier, it is not possible to see in British profiles of either peat or lake sediments, a lower boundary to the Sub-Boreal period as a climatic entity, its upper limit is very clearly defined in very many of the bogs of Great Britain, which seem to have had a period of slow growth and formation of highly humified peat, during the second part of the Sub-Boreal period. This type of growth was apparently brought to an end by a fairly sudden change in character of the peat of these bogs, and this change has been dated by radiocarbon in many parts of England and Wales to the centuries between 800 and 500 B.C.—that is, to the end of the Bronze Age and opening of the Iron Age. From the extent of upland settlement in England and Wales during the Bronze Age, particularly on Dartmoor and in the Lake District, it would seem that the climate may have been warmer and drier than that of today—that is, nearer to conditions resembling the Continental Sub-Boreal than to our present highly oceanic climate. In Fenland, the marginal areas became drier, and were colonised by pine during this period. The main evidence for a deterioration in climate towards the end of the Bronze Age comes from peat stratigraphy, and it must be said at once that this evidence, though so clear in parts of Great Britain, cannot be found in Ireland. In Ireland there is evidence for renewed impetus in the growth of the raised bogs and blanket peat from about 2000 B.C. onwards, and after that no single horizon in the Irish pollen diagrams points clearly to a synchronous climatic change. It would seem that there the climate has been one of steadily high oceanicity.

Recurrence surfaces

In England and Wales, on the other hand, the raised bogs which began to grow in Atlantic times were apparently growing very slowly in parts of the later Sub-Boreal (Bronze Age). Many of them became dry enough to become colonised by ling (*Calluna*), pine (where that tree survived) and birch, these plants replacing the peat-forming communities which were probably mainly *Sphagnum* and *Eriophorum*. Plate 77 in Tansley illustrates sections in raised bogs which show this. The highly humified peat of this "standstill" phase is possibly now incomplete, since peat erosion may have occurred during the "standstill" phase. In very many English and Welsh bogs, the vertical sections left by peat-cutters show that on top of this dark, highly humified peat, which is without structure, there is a sudden change to a much fresher peat, in which the individual *Sphagnum* plants which form it can still be distinguished from each other; that is, the upper peat is unhumified. At the junction between the two peats can often be found recognisable remains of plants now known to live in pools on wet bog surfaces—among these are a sedge, *Carex limosa*, and *Scheuchzeria palustris*, with aquatic species of *Sphagnum*, such as *Sphagnum cuspidatum*, and *S. imbricatum* which is a tussock-forming species very characteristic of this peat. In some English and Welsh bogs only one major transition of this type occurs; in others there may be several, but often the lowest is the most intense and easy to recognise. The transition between humified and unhumified peat marks a Recurrence Surface. The plants of the actively growing bog surface represented by the unhumified peat form the Regeneration Complex.

The main Recurrence Surface recognised in English and Welsh raised bogs is often called the *Grenz-horizont* or Boundary Horizon, as it seems to correspond with this phenomenon in German raised bogs described by Weber. It is, in the British zonations scheme, ued to define the pollen zone-boundary VIIb/VIII, which corresponds with the Sub-Boreal/Sub-Atlantic transition. The position is complicated, however, by the existence of other recurrence surfaces, and sometimes it is difficult to determine accurately the position of a recurrence surface, in the materal brought up in the sampling chamber of a Hiller-type borer. This may have led to some contradictory evidence about recurrence surfaces where no exposed peat face is available; it is true to say that not all recurrence surfaces are as clearly defined as the classic Weber pattern, and there is still discussion among ecologists as to whether every example of a recurrence surface can be interpreted as a response to a change in water-level brought about by increased oceanicity of climate. The Swedish ecologist Granlund observed five distinct recurrence surfaces in the bogs of south Sweden, and assigned dates to these on the evidence available before the application of the radiocarbon dating technique. The middle and most pronounced of Granlund's five recurrence surfaces is equated with Weber's *Grenz-horizont*. Granlund's theory was that a raised bog could grow upwards only to a certain limiting height before drainage would initiate retardation of peat growth, and then would cease to grow until the next general shift towards increased oceanicity of climate produced a recurrence surface. This theory has now been discarded by most ecologists in Britain, since the very great size of many British bogs makes it impossible to believe that an increase in height of a few feet at the centre could critically affect drainage.

As far as the author is aware, no radiocarbon-dated evidence has been produced in Britain which unequivocally supports Granlund's supposed increases in oceanicity at 2300 B.C. and 1200 B.C. Several radiocarbon dates put the beginning of the major growth of Irish peat, both in raised and blanket bogs, at about 2000 B.C. It is likely, therefore, that throughout Sub-Boreal times there were periods when the ratio between precipitation and evaporation increased, and that the exact way in which this affected the rate of peat formation varied from one climatic region to another, between Ireland on the one hand and eastern Scandinavia on the other.

The phenomenon of the major recurrence surface in Great Britain has been studied in relation to the Late Bronze Age trackways, which have been discovered in many raised bogs. These consist of "corduroy roads" of logs, sometimes still bearing the characteristic blade-marks of the Late Bronze Age axes with which they were fashioned. These trackways are usually in a very good state of preservation, and appear to have had comparatively little wear before being overwhelmed and preserved by the rapid growth of peat.

In the great raised bogs of the Somerset Levels, six of these trackways have been dated by radiocarbon, after detailed pollen analysis by Godwin and his co-workers had established them to be of comparable position in the vegetation sequence. All of them appeared to have been constructed to keep open communications, between hill ridges on which settlements appear to have become isolated by the increasing impassability caused by rising water level in the bogs. All the trackways were laid on the surface of a very dark, highly humified, *Sphagnum–Calluna–Eriophorum* peat, and were overlain by fresh peat composed of *Cladium mariscus* and the moss *Hypnum*, which represents the type of vegetation likely to be produced on a peat surface flooded by calcareous water—in this area, probably from the limestone area of the Mendip and Polden hills. The dates obtained for the trackways on this recurrence surface in the Somerset bogs all lie between 450 and 900 B.C., which is certainly Late Bronze Age, and is in accord with the conception of the main climatic deterioration as occurring at the Bronze Age/Iron Age transition.

Three other similar trackways were dated in Cambridge and gave results within the same period, one from Cambridgeshire, one from Lincolnshire, and one from Pilling Moss, one of the great raised bogs of the Lancashire plain.

The sequence at Tregaron Bog

In the three large raised bogs of the complex at Tregaron, in Cardiganshire, shown in Plate 9, a well developed *Grenz-horizont* is found, separating lower, highly humified peat from upper, moderately humified fresh *Sphagnum* peat. Turner has shown that the radiocarbon dates placed the *Grenz-horizont* between *c.* 1000 B.C. and 700 B.C. (each date the average of two determinations and $\pm$ 110), and suggests that there was some erosion at that level before the fresh peat began to form. A higher layer of humified peat showing a minor fluctuation, or "retardation layer", where the peat growth slowed down, was dated to between 1182 and 1472 A.D. There was a very great contrast between accumulation rates within the post-Grenz, or Sub-Atlantic peat, all composed of *Sphagnum imbricatum*. From the Grenz at *c.* 696 B.C. to *c.* 400 B.C., the rate of growth of the very fresh unhumified peat must have been of the order of one centimetre in three years, but the more humified peat above, from 404 B.C. until 1182 A.D., had grown only at a mean rate of one centimetre in fifty years. By very detailed pollen analyses, Dr Turner was able to show that the record of local human activity preserved in the pollen of the Tregaron peats indicates temporary periods of partial clearance, until a short period of extensive clearance occurred just before 404 B.C. During the Late Bronze Age period of small temporary clearances, the radiocarbon dates in this Tregaron profile are sufficiently close together to date the successive phases of a single clearance. The actual disforestation seems to have occupied about 10 years, and then an interval of about 15 years elapsed, and then regeneration of the birch began and lasted for about 30 years. By about 404 B.C. this period of shifting clearances had been changed to a system of more open grassland by the short period of intensive forest clearance, and the long period of pastoral farming which followed coincides with the occupation of the Tregaron area by Celtic tribes, which are known to have pastured large flocks and herds. This pastoral period ends with a significant change which was dated to 1182 A.D., where a shift to predominantly arable farming is indicated by the appearance in the pollen diagram of *Artemisia*, and genera of the families Chenopodiaceae, Ranunculaceae, and Compositae. This coincides in a striking way with the known settlement of Cistercian monks at Strata Florida nearby in 1164 A.D.; the monks are known to have stimulated agriculture and to have grown barley and oats extensively on their lowland granges.

North-western England

In the raised bogs around Morecambe Bay, Smith, Oldfield and Statham have been able to demonstrate a comparable link between vegetation history as recorded in pollen diagrams and local historical geography, though without the precision given to Turner's work by her close series of radiocarbon dates.

The vegetation change which Oldfield and Statham link with the twelfth-century establishment of Cistercian monasteries in the north-west is a great extension of cleared land, which they attribute to the sheep-farming which the Cistercians are well known to have developed from Furness Abbey, and

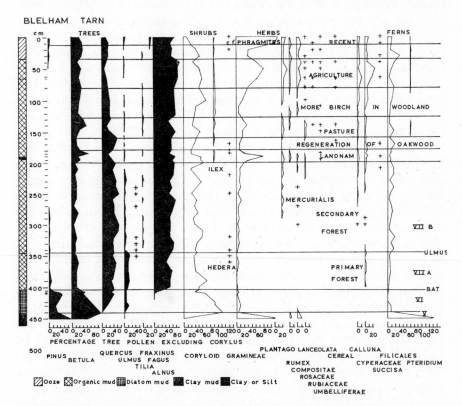

Figure 22. The history of oakwood; a pollen diagram from Blelham Tarn, N. Lancs. Reproduced by permission of the Royal Society from a paper by the author in *Proc. Roy. Soc.*, **B161**, 1965.

which certainly must have resulted in much clearing of local woodlands for more pastures. The extension of arable farming in the north-west seems to have occurred in two main episodes, one dating from the level of a retardation layer in Helsington Moss which has a radiocarbon date of *c.* 436 A.D., and which is thought to correlate with the late- and immediately post-Roman period, a time when the north-west of England saw an extension of farming activity—and the second, which is fairly high in the profile, is attributed to enclosure and settlement of the monastic lands by small yeomen farmers, with consequently more intensive cultivation, after the dissolution of Furness Abbey in 1537.

In the central Lake District, it has been possible to show that, after the Neolithic episodes which have been dated to just before 3000 B.C., more permanent forest clearance differs from place to place in a manner consistent with the distribution of traces of later populations. In those parts of the uplands where there are stone circles and burial cairns of Bronze Age type, there are signs of pastoral activity at a corresponding level in the pollen diagrams, with replacement of much woodland by grassland and heather moor, now dated to *c*. 1080 B.C. (Fig. 15). A later type of episode, now dated to between 250 A.D. and 450 A.D., corresponding more nearly with Turner's "extensive clearances", is accompanied by cereal pollen, and corresponds in distribution with the "British settlements" of hut circles, few of which have yet been archaeologically dated, and hill farms of approximately Romano-British type, but with a native (Celtic or "Brigantian") form of land use, very different from the Romano-British farms of the lowland zone of Britain. The retardation layers from Tregaron Bog and from Helsington Moss, with their radiocarbon dates of 404 A.D. and 436 A.D. respectively, are very suggestive of a period of drier climate about this time, and this would of course explain why this period saw the cultivation of cereals at higher altitudes in the Lake District than before or since. In the valleys of the southern Lake District the woodland seems to have persisted through prehistoric time with no more than very temporary disturbance, but a severe and partially permanent deforestation episode rather high in the profiles is correlated in distribution (from place-name evidence) with the settlement of Vikings from Norway and from the Norse settlements in Ireland and the Isle of Man, during the ninth and tenth centuries A.D.: see Fig. 22, Blelham Tarn. Historical tradition blames the Vikings for destruction by burning of some of the Scottish forests, in the area of the north-west coast of Scotland which still bears traces in place-names of the Viking settlement, and it may well be that future research in this area will be able to show whether or not this is true.

Climatic change in the Sub-Atlantic period

Godwin's zonation of the Post-glacial profiles from Britain is based on the conception that a zone-boundary should indicate a synchronous climatic change—though of course the details of the vegetation change which results from the climatic change will be expected to vary from one site to another. Originally, the zone-boundary VIIb/VIII was drawn, for south-eastern England, where the beech (*Fagus*) and the hornbeam (*Carpinus*) first appear as a continuous curve in pollen diagrams—that is, at least one grain of each occurs in every sample if a total of 150 tree grains is counted. It was soon found that this basis of zonation could not be used in northern and western Britain, because these two trees did not penetrate very far northwards or westwards as native species. Neither reached Ireland at all, and in this they resemble the lime. It is still far from clear where exactly the beech and horn-beam were growing (though they are known to have been present in Hants) after they had, as is believed, reached south-eastern England before Britain was cut off from Continental Europe, by about 5500 B.C., and before their apparently rather sudden expansion at the end of the Sub-Boreal period, at about 500 B.C. As we have seen, the climatic shift at about 500 B.C. was a deterioration, in the sense that peat began to grow more quickly and water-levels on the bogs rose. Probably the climate became both cooler and wetter. It is difficult to see how such a change would favour beech and hornbeam, which are continental rather than oceanic in their distribution, so it would seem that anthropogenic factors may have been involved. This will be con-sidered further in Chapter 11, when discussing the history of beechwoods. The hornbeam, *Carpinus betulus*, was characteristic of the corresponding stage of the last interglacial, that is, between the deposits of the climatic optimum stage and the later stages of the interglacial which were dominated by conifer-ous forests; its pollen is present in quantity in deposits of this stage of the Eemian Interglacial in Denmark, and in the corresponding deposits of the Ipswichian Interglacial, at Histon Road, Cambridge.

The other trees which were at one time considered to have responded to the climatic deterioration at the zone boundary VIIb/VIII are the birch and the lime, but it now seems very probable that both the increase in birch and decrease or disappearance of the lime at this horizon depend primarily on the human history of the area, and are not so nearly synchronous from place to place as they would be if the cause had been primarily climatic. Nevertheless, the cooler and wetter climate of the Sub-Atlantic period must have tended to suppress the lime still further, and we have already considered how the less exacting birch would tend to increase under conditions unfavour-able to more exacting trees.

Betula species respond very quickly to anthropogenic disturbance of the forest. Birch is the first tree to spread by seed into newly cleared areas, it springs up again first after a clearance by fire, and it tolerates soils which have been either impoverished by primitive agriculture or podsolised by the effects of a wet climate at higher altitudes, or—like the Tertiary sands of the London and Hampshire basins, are poor and infertile by nature, and so likely to have been lightly covered by trees during the Atlantic period, and deforested in the early stages of prehistoric clearances. All these characteristics of the birch tend towards the increase in its relative abundance as clearance and settlement progress through prehistory and history. It seems quite possible that when the horizons of the first "revertence" of the birch in Britain are closely dated, they will prove to be non-synchronous, and so will make the use of the birch curve as an indicator of the zone boundary unsound.

The chief process which has tended to *reduce* birch in the later part of the Post-glacial period is the destruction of high-level birch forest, and probably much lowland birch forest in the North-west Highlands, by the Sub-Atlantic extension of blanket peat. Over some areas of the Pennines, peat growth was at a standstill during the Sub-Boreal period, but was renewed as the climate became wetter and cooler, when great extension of the mantle of blanket peat over upland birch forest in parts of the north of England took place. The entombed remains of this birch forest constitute one very obvious piece of evidence for a higher tree limit in the past than that which operates today. The former tree limit indicated by the buried timber suggests a tree-line at *c*. 2500 feet, compared with about 1750 feet for birch today, in the northern Pennines.

The processes by which this change from forest on rather acid soils to blanket peat may come about were discussed in a paper by Iversen (1964) on "Retrogressive vegetational succession in the Post-glacial". The change involved is in his opinion due entirely to leaching of the soil. In the particular Danish forest which he discusses, the severity of the leaching is due to the sandy texture and poverty in bases of the mineral soil. On British mountains, the severity of the leaching is due to the excessively high rainfall. Discussing the accumulation of mor humus on top of forest soils, Iversen says "The formation of mor is primarily a function of the high acidity, which prevents the growth of those micro-organisms which attack pollen exines and other particularly resistant organic debris. Normally there is no deficiency in oxygen (Romell, 1922) but deep mor layers, as well as the humus-iron-pan, may prevent vertical drainage and thus reduces aeration, and, in moist climates, accelerate the growth of the mor, or even produce swamping. The blanket bogs of the British Isles are outstanding examples of this".

Certainly the soil of these buried birch forests on the Lake District mountains, from 1200 feet upwards, has much in common with the deep mor layers described by Iversen from Draved in Jutland. The old soil contains abundant pollen in an excellent state of preservation, and like the Jutland mor, it can be shown to have built up in temporal succession, with no mixing. The high acidity of the mor would inhibit earthworms. No iron-pan layer is visible in the soil profile below the blanket bog, but as Iversen points out, the very thickness of the accumulating mor "prevents vertical drainage", and so in the Lake District, with a rainfall of about 120 inches a year, brings about swamping of the surface. This produces an environment where few if any bacteria will grow, and so practically no breakdown of plant residues results, and peat begins to accumulate. Figure 23 illustrates a section through the peat on the fells above Wrynose Pass in the Lake District, where buried birchwood has been dated by radio-carbon to 3890 B.P. This date shows that replacement of high-level forest by peat had begun long before the opening of the Sub-Atlantic period here, as on high parts of the northern Pennines (Johnson and Dunham 1963). Over much of the Pennines, however, a great acceleration in the rate of growth of the peat has been attributed by Conway to climatic deterioration at the opening of the Sub-Atlantic period.

Evidence from Ireland

In the Irish bogs there are many recurrence surfaces of a minor type, but no single example which can be interpreted as indicating a synchronous renewal of rapid growth of peat because of a climatic shift towards greater oceanicity. Mitchell has therefore abandoned any attempt to draw a synchronous zone boundary at the Sub-Boreal/Sub-Atlantic contact, and instead proposes a zonation scheme based on a synthesis of the vegetation changes caused by man. From the opening of the Neolithic period at *c.* 5000 B.P. until 300 A.D., he considers that the vegetation of Ireland was affected primarily by man, and that peat growth had become general in parts of the west by 2000 B.C.,

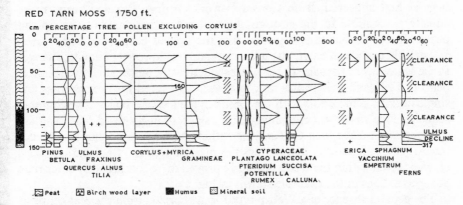

RED TARN MOSS 1750 ft.

Figure 23. The formation of blanket bog; a pollen diagram from Red Tarn Moss, Langdale, Westmorland. Reproduced by permission of the Royal Society from a paper by the author in *Proc. Roy. Soc.,* **B161,** 1965. (Wood from 100 cm. dated by radiocarbon to 1940 B.C.)

and that the peat-covered areas thereafter steadily expanded. The whole long section of time from 5000 B.P. to 300 A.D. constitutes his "pagan period", which includes the Neolithic and Bronze Age types of farming: see Fig. 21. In Ireland there was no clear change in land use at the end of the Bronze Age, and the extension of farming which was such a strong feature of the Iron Age in many parts of Great Britain was quite absent from Ireland. Instead there was a great increase in the amount of cleared ground, and corresponding diminution in elm and ash (the trees of the better soils) at about 300 A.D., which Mitchell attributes to the beginning of the Christian era in Ireland and the stimulus to agriculture under the influence of Celtic monasticism. The increase in proportion of birch pollen in Irish diagrams appears to date from the reduced farming activity at the end of this monastic period, and to be wholly due to human destruction of the primary forest followed by secondary birch on exploited land. This provides further evidence for the viewpoint that the "revertence" of the birch curve is an anthropogenic, and not primarily a climatic, effect. It is of course impossible to know what the course of forest history would have been in north-west Europe if man had not been present, but where the course of the birch curve is different in two neighbouring islands which have had a different human history, then it is at least likely that the climatic control has not been of primary importance.

Recent evidence from blanket peats

Much of the early evidence from pollen analysis on Sub-Atlantic vegetation history came from the peat of lowland raised bogs. The climatic shift to cooler and wetter conditions indicated by the peat stratigraphy of these bogs at first appeared, from Conway's work on deep Pennine peats, to be equally perceptible in the stratigraphy and pollen sequence of the upland peats. It was at that time expected that the upland peats would have been susceptible to the same climatic influences and would record climatic changes in the same way as the raised bogs. Subsequent work on the shallower blanket peats of Highland Britain has not, however, discovered in these profiles any single horizon comparable with the Grenz in the lowland bogs. The common sequence is of wood peat containing birch, alder, or in Scotland pine, overlain by *Eriophorum-Sphagnum-Calluna* peat within which no clear major Recurrence Surface can be found, though minor ones may be present. Radiocarbon dates on wood from within the wood peat have proved to be considerably older than 800–500 B.C., as in the example shown in Fig. 23.

The general absence of a Weber-type Grenz horizon from the blanket peats of Highland Britain agrees with evidence from Ireland. In all these areas of highly oceanic climate there is no record of major climatic change, but only of conditions favourable to peat formation since long before the opening of the Sub-Atlantic period. Episodes of human interference with vegetation have now been recorded and dated from blanket peat in many parts of Britain. Dr Moore (1973) working in Wales has postulated that the vegetational regression from upland woodland to bog was accelerated by forest clearance and stock grazing. (See also Chap. 11.)

Plate II. Wistman's Wood, Dartmoor. Relict *Quercus robur* woodland, with a sapling of rowan (*Sorbus aucuparia*). M. C. F. Proctor.

Plate 12. Irish bog on the central plain; peat utilisation. J. E. Lousley.

Plate 13. Moughton Fell, West Yorkshire, with Pen-y-Ghent in the distance. Juniper scrub. A peaty hollow with *Empetrum* in the middle distance. M. C. F. Proctor.

Plate 14. Glenridding. Westmorland, looking up to Brown Cove, with Catchedicam on the left. Juniper scrub. M. C. F. Proctor.

Plate 15. Grizedale, Westmorland, looking up to Dollywaggon Pike. Mountain grasslands grazed by sheep, formerly forest. On the steep slopes the grassland is of *Agrostis-Festuca-Deschampsia flexuosa* with abundant *Vaccinium*, and on the moraines, visible in the high corrie, and on the floor of the main valley, the grassland is of *Nardus stricta*. M. C. F. Proctor.

Plate 16. *Salix herbacea* (Least Willow), Ben Nevis. M. C. F. Proctor.

Plate 17. *Betula nana* (Dwarf Birch), Abisko, Sweden. M. C. F. Proctor.

Plate 18. *Dryas octopetala* (Mountain Avens), with leaves of *Alchemilla alpina* (Alpine Lady's Mantle), near Braemar, Aberdeenshire. M. C. F. Proctor.

Plate 19. *Helianthemum canum* (Rock-rose), County Clare. M. C. F. Proctor.

Plate 20. *Dryas-Empetrum* heath on the Burren, County Clare. M. C. F. Proctor.

Plate 21. *Lycopodium selago* (Fir-tree Club Moss), Dartmoor. M. C. F. Proctor.

9 Later changes in vegetation, and species introduced into the flora by Man

Artificial habitats created by Man; the expansion into them of native and introduced species

SINCE, as we have seen, forest was the natural vegetation of nearly all Britain before the arrival of Neolithic man, most British grasslands and heaths are "artificial" habitats. Over the course of millennia, however, characteristic and stable plant communities have become established in them, to such an extent that we now regard them as types of British vegetation. The truly artificial habitats which men have created are those where no stable plant communities can form.

So long as agriculture was primitive and shifting, the ground disturbed by cultivation must have reverted quite soon to scrub and then to forest again when the cultivators moved on. This is the vegetation sequence shown in Turner's "small temporary clearances", and as her diagram shows (Fig. 20), this was the prevailing method of land use in much of Britain until the opening of the Iron Age; it is believed that the cultivation was done with primitive implements such as digging sticks and hoes (possibly resembling the Hebridean caschrom). It was only when the introduction of ploughs and, later, some knowledge of manuring techniques made it possible to keep ground under more permanent cultivation, that the "artificial" habitat of bare and continuously disturbed soils came into being on any considerable scale. The Celtic peoples of England and Wales seem to have practised a more advanced technique of farming, from about 400 B.C. onwards, and it is recorded in written history that when the Romans arrived in Britain, there was much corn grown in south-eastern England, that some was exported, and that the Britons manured their fields with chalk. The cornfield as a habitat for plants able to colonise bare soil, and to survive cultivation practices by annual renewal by seeding, must have come into existence during the pre-Roman Iron Age.

Bare soil had last been available as a "natural" habitat in Britain during the Late-glacial period. It has been shown in Chapter 4 how there were many plants in the Late-glacial flora which were very well adapted to succeed in such a habitat, and how they flourished in that time when great areas of soil seem to have been kept open—that is, not covered by a continuous plant carpet—by frost action, and when the temperatures were too low to permit the growth of trees (many of the plants of open habitats are light-demanding and cannot flourish in shade). Among plants widely and abundantly recorded from the Late-glacial period and then almost completely suppressed by forest, until man began to cultivate the soil, the genera *Rumex* (docks) (Plate 28) and *Artemisia* (wormwood, mugwort) have already been cited as examples. Other probably "native" weeds include the cornflower (*Centaurea cyanus*), pollen of which has been identified from Late-glacial deposits, though it is still uncertain whether this plant, whose natural habitat is now rather dry Mediterranean hillsides, and steppes, survived the forest period in Britain, or died out and was re-introduced with seed corn by Neolithic or later farmers. These genera, with genera of the Compositae and Caryophyllaceae, are found, in the form of pollen grains, dating from clearance horizons during the pre-historic period—see Fig. 17, but must have increased considerably when permanent arable fields came into being.

Another category of plants now growing as weeds, and possibly including truly native species, are those known to have been utilised as subsidiary foods by prehistoric and later men. These include such plants as the Fat Hen (*Chenopodium album*) which has been recorded from the Late-glacial, and others found for the first time in association with Neolithic remains, such as the Black bindweed (*Polygonum convolvulus*), Good King Henry (*Chenopodium bonus-henricus*) and the Onion couch (*Arrhenatherum elatius* var. *tuberosum*).

The "ruderal" or wayside habitat is one which must have come into being with the earliest forest clearances. Salisbury points out in his discussion of this habitat that it is really an extension of the natural habitat of the woodland margin, where light-demanding plants could flourish under the shelter, and "annual surface-dressing of organic material", provided by the adjacent woodlands. During the long prehistoric period of shifting cultivation, this habitat must have been continually renewed as new clearings were made, and at the same time trackways, however impermanent, would keep open further manifestations of this habitat. Waybread (*Plantago major*) is an example of a category of herbs which can endure much trampling, and clearly expanded very extensively into the trackway habitat, in prehistoric times, after having been almost completely suppressed since the end of the Late-glacial period, when it was common.

Later, the tracks between more permanent settlements would serve as channels along which introduced species could spread rapidly. Both Godwin and Salisbury have emphasised how the Roman road system in England and Wales must have provided ideal conditions for the rapid spread of introduced plants (compare Table XIII, Godwin 1956), because the roads were constructed with sloping embankments which offered many miles of open ground, available for plant colonisation, and the heavy traffic along the roads would provide a continuous source of fruits and seeds in process of dispersal, particularly of cornfield weeds, since there was much movement of imported corn for army rations. Among the very long list of weeds and ruderals which Godwin quotes as recorded for the first time in Post-glacial Britain in Romano-British times are those familiar cornfield weeds the Corn Marigold (*Chrysanthemum segetum*), the Corn cockle (*Agrostemma githago*) and the Scarlet Pimpernel (*Anagallis arvensis*). This rapid spread of introduced plants along highways of communication has of course been paralleled in our own time by the very rapid spread of the Oxford Ragwort (*Senecio squalidus*) from the Oxford Botanic Garden, along railway tracks, and the equally rapid spread along roadsides and farm tracks of the Pineapple Weed (*Matricaria matricarioides*) (Plate 30), a plant native to north-east Asia which reached Britain, apparently via America, in the nineteenth century, and has had two periods of very rapid spread, one in the early twentieth century and one since the Second World War. A further example of the spread into new habitats provided by man was the invasion of bombed sites by the Fireweed (*Epilobium* or *Chamaenerion angustifolium*), a plant which was common during Late-glacial times in Britain, but was of comparatively restricted distribution until widespread bombing provided suitable new open habitats for colonisation by the very efficiently dispersed seeds of this plant.

The rapid spread of ruderals among land plants has been paralleled by the dispersion along canals and shipping routes of certain water plants introduced from North America. Of these, the Water fern (*Azolla filiculoides*) is of especial interest, because it was a native plant in Britain during the Cromerian and Hoxnian Interglacials, hundreds of thousands of years ago, and is one of the plants which apparently did not return after the post-Hoxnian glaciation. The Canadian pondweed (*Elodea canadensis*) is another native of the North American flora which flourishes in the present climate of Britain; after its introduction in the early nineteenth century it spread very quickly, especially along the canal system. The Rice Grass (*Spartina townsendii*) is a plant of tidal mud flats, which arose during the nineteenth century as a hybrid, the result of a cross between the native salt-marsh species *Spartina maritima* and the American *Spartina alterniflora*, which was introduced into Southampton Water by shipping from North America, in the early years of the century. By 1870 the new plant was first noticed, and it then spread with hybrid vigour into vast areas of mud flats along the south coast of England. In this example, it is the origin of the plant—the bringing together of its parents—which was "artificial"; the habitat is a natural one which had hitherto not been fully occupied.

Permanent forest clearance—heavy ploughs and arable fields
(i) Celtic and Roman Britain—highland and lowland zones

The first "extensive clearance" at Tregaron dates from about 400 B.C., and Turner has found the same record of change in land use, at roughly the same time, in Somerset and Yorkshire. This corresponds very well with archaeologicial dates for the coming of the Celtic people of the Iron Age. At Tregaron, the long period of permanent clearance of the forest which followed the extensive clearance was predominantly pastoral, as Turner has been able to demonstrate convincingly from detailed pollen analysis of the vegetation. This presents a botanical analysis of Iron Age land use in the Highland zone of Britain which corresponds very well with Stuart Piggott's archaeological analysis of native economies in North Britain (1961). Both authors (see Turner, Fig. 20) agree that there is much evidence to suggest that in the pre-Roman Iron Age, and at the time of the Roman conquest, corn growing was confined to the Lowland zone of Britain, south and east of the Jurassic ridge, roughly the Severn-Humber line. The only possible exceptions seem to be a few isolated areas, in Anglesey and one or two other parts of North Wales, the Derbyshire and Craven limestone uplands, parts of north-east Yorkshire and Cumberland, where traces of "Celtic field systems" of possibly pre-Roman date survive. But the evidence provided by the distribution of grain storage pits is that north and west of the Severn–Humber line there was no systematic provision for the storage of grain, and so, presumably, little corn was grown. This agrees with Turner's botanical evidence, as set out in Fig. 20. Piggot states that "all finds of carbonised grain from Brigantia or farther north are of Roman or later date . . . There seems then singularly little archaeological evidence for anything more than a continuance of Bronze Age agricultural techniques, in what we call for convenience the Brigantian area, until the introduction of more advanced techniques after the Roman crossing of the Humber". All the evidence from Highland Britain presents a picture of the invading tribes of Celts, who came to occupy the British hills, not as settled farming people but as almost wholly pastoral, possessing great herds of cattle, some sheep, and possibly acting as the main breeders of chariot ponies, using metal axes to clear permanently great areas of forest which became grassland for grazing, but not cultivating cereals to any extent. The Roman record that the Britons of this region subsisted on meat and milk, and not bread, is in agreement with this conclusion.

In Lowland Britain, south and east of the Jurassic ridge, the Celtic economy was very different. The clearest picture of it comes from the farm of Little

Woodbury, on the chalk south-west of Salisbury, where evidence has come to light on the way of life of the farmers who occupied the site from about 300 B.C. until the Roman conquest. The site represents a single stockaded farm, which, from the extent of the provision for storing grain in underground pits, seems to have cultivated about 15–20 acres of arable land, with provision for grazing sheep and some cattle on what seems to have been by then established grassland on the surrounding chalk downs. The seed corn was stored in small granaries on posts, and the rest of the crop was apparently parched, in ovens made of chalk cob, and then stored in the underground pits for winter and spring food. It would be farmers of this sort whom Pliny described as manuring their fields with chalk, so they were conscious of the need to maintain the fertility of the soil. The acreage calculated above allows for a proportion of the fields to lie fallow each year. This type of farming seems to have continued through the Roman occupation, and these fallow fields would be invaded by the alien weeds which were doubtless imported with rations of corn for the legionaries, and dispersed along the developing network of new roads.

The direct effects of the Roman occupiers on the farming and vegetation of Britain, though small in comparison with their military and urban constructions, were twofold. There is evidence that corn-growing was extended and encouraged, especially in Fenland, where a great increase in farmed land dates from this period. Here it is clear that wheat was grown. In many parts, the Romans encouraged the growing of rye. It seems likely too that some increase in corn-growing in the more favourable parts of the Highland zone extended the acreage of cultivated land; pollen-analytical evidence for this in north-west England has been described in the previous chapter. Secondly, in the Romanised parts of the Lowland zone, where the villa estates, often of considerable size, were worked by labourers or slaves, the Romans introduced many new crop plants, including the vine, mulberry, walnut, fig, plum and medlar, the pea, the radish and many culinary herbs such as fennel and dill. (Cf. Godwin, 1956, Table XIII.) Some of the introduced pot-herbs of this period have found conditions in cultivated ground so favourable that they have become serious weeds—the ground elder (*Aegopodium podagraria*) is a notorious example—and some have become naturalised members of the British flora, like alexanders (*Smyrnium olusatrum*), Plate 29. Finally, though as yet there is no dated botanical evidence to document this, the Roman descriptions of the importance of the wool trade and weaving to the Britons of this period suggest that sheep were kept under both Highland and Lowland zone farming systems, and this must have tended towards further extension of grassland at the expense of forest. Further inroads on surviving forests were made in areas, such as the Weald, where extensive iron-smelting had begun at about this time.

Anglo-Saxon and Scandinavian settlement

The evidence for farms of Romano-British date has survived mainly on lighter upland soils. Traces in the valleys may well have been obliterated by later ploughing but great areas of heavy clays in the Midlands, the Weald and parts of East Anglia must still have been covered by dense unbroken oak forests. The plough that was in use in Celtic and Romano-British times was of comparatively simple plan, often with no device for turning a heavy sod. When Roman Britain came to an end, the potentially fertile lowland clays, still covered with forest, were the areas on which the land-hungry Angles and Saxons were to settle. It has been suggested that their introduction of the heavy eight-ox plough was an innovation in agricultural practice. The fertile valley soils could now be broken up for cultivation, and the long straight-sided acre strips of the Anglo-Saxon settlements formed the basis of the large open fields of the mediaeval villages. Only in the Highland zone did the irregular pattern of the Celtic fields remain. As yet, there is no detailed work in historical botany on the effect on the weed flora of this change in agricultural practice, but it may well have been considerable. At the end of the Romano-British period, the Fenland was inundated by a great marine transgression, and much of the fertile cornland which the Romans had developed became once more a waterlogged swamp. The deposits of this marine incursion form the Upper Silt, now some of the most agriculturally productive soils in the country.

At Old Buckenham Mere in East Anglia, Godwin has been able to show how a great extension of arable farming in Anglo-Saxon times has left traces in the pollen record. From historical sources, it is known that the Angles who penetrated up the valleys of the Midland rivers from the Wash had made permanent settlements by the end of the fifth century, like Rockingham, and Bringhurst on its hill ("the wooded knoll of Bryni's people"), by the Welland, and that by the eleventh century there were still great tracts of uncleared forest between these rivers, like Bruneswald between the Ouse and the Nene, which sheltered the Saxon outlaw Hereward—but there is no evidence of the stages by which forest destruction had proceeded through the intervening six hundred years. The Danish invasions of the ninth century and the establishment of new villages by Danish-speaking settlers in the Danelaw must have accelerated the destruction of the oak forests. In the hills of north-west England there are comparatively few Anglian place-names, and it would seem that a Celtic (Brigantian) type of land use continued on the lower uplands of the Lake District and parts of the Pennines until after the valleys were invaded and settled by Norwegian Vikings, probably via their settlements in Ireland and the Isle of Man, in the ninth and tenth centuries. The contrasted history of the uplands and lowlands in the southern Lake District can be seen by comparing Fig. 15 (Seathwaite Tarn) with the history of the lowland woods round Blelham Tarn which is discussed during the consideration of the history of the British woodlands, in the following chapter (see Fig. 22).

In south-east Britain, the period of change from the cultivation of the upland chalk during the Celtic Iron Age and Roman times, to the settlement of the valley clays by Anglo-Saxons and Danish immigrants, may well have been the time when the beech established itself as the dominant tree of chalk country. We know from pollen evidence that it is a recent dominant in the woodlands. In the politically unsettled conditions which followed the end of Roman Britain, much cultivated farmland on the chalk must have gone out of cultivation. It would then pass, by a succession of plant communities or "sere", through scrub to some sort of woodland, and possibly the beech was able to expand into this habitat and establish itself, though previously it had been unable to compete with oak as a forest-former. That part of the upland chalk and oolitic limestone which continued to be grazed, after the long period of prehistoric and Celtic occupation, would be the fore-runner of our present calcareous grasslands.

Norman and mediaeval England

The Norman Royal Forests, of which the New Forest is the outstanding survivor, were forests in the legal rather than the botanical sense—they were areas subject to a special law, the aim of which was the preservation of the king's hunting. The kings gave protection to animals of the chase, particularly deer, in these areas, and William I is known to have evicted the villagers of established agricultural settlements, at least in the New Forest. This procedure would encourage the reversion of arable land to scrub and so to secondary forest. Many areas were described in documents of this period as "waste", and the actual vegetation of the waste is not fully known. Much of it was probably either degeneration stages in natural forest under heavy grazing by cattle and pigs, preventing regeneration of the trees, or stages in the reversion of formerly cultivated land to scrub—again with grazing pressure sufficiently heavy to prevent tree seedlings from reaching maturity. The extent of the "waste" was of course very great in those areas most devastated by fighting, and such episodes as the "harrying of the north" in 1069 must have allowed many square miles of fertile ploughland to go out of cultivation, and revert to scrub, at least temporarily. From the Domesday survey, it would seem that high forest occupied considerably more land then than it does now. One of the most important ecological changes in this period was the introduction of the rabbit, which as a grazing factor and preventer of natural regeneration of trees was to rival the sheep in future centuries.

Agricultural development in England and Wales was stimulated in many parts by the foundation of about fifty Cistercian monasteries in the years between 1127 and 1152. The Cistercians were famous as efficient farmers and estate managers, and their houses were founded in rural surroundings far away from towns. Turner's pollen diagram from Tregaron shows how the plant indicators of arable farming—pollen of cultivated cereals and weeds —are first found at a level dated by radiocarbon to within a few years of the foundation of the nearby Cistercian house of Strata Florida, and it is clear that in this area the monks must have encouraged cultivation both of their own lands and those of their tenant farmers. The great Cistercian house of Furness was given by Stephen a grant of land which by about 1163 had been extended to include most of the eastern part of the present Furness district, and subsequently the Furness monks added to their Lake District lands by purchase. In the botanical record from both High and Low Furness, in lake sediments and in raised bogs, there is evidence for rapid expansion of grassland and decrease in woodland at a level which seems to correspond approximately with this time, though as yet this period of clearance has not been dated by radiocarbon, as it has at Strata Florida. The written records of the abbeys confirm that the monks were sheep farmers and wool merchants on a vast scale, and in northern England must have stimulated the conversion of great tracts of woodland into grassland. Figure 24 is a map of the extent of the English forests remaining by about 1250, reproduced from Darby.

Apart from the direct influence of the Cistercians, the process of extending clearances for tillage—assarting—must have proceeded through the centuries which followed the Norman Conquest. At some time during the Middle Ages, the remaining oakwoods began to be managed as "coppice with standards"—the fully grown standard oaks providing large timber, and the repeatedly coppiced lower layer, mainly of oak and hazel, providing poles for a variety of woodland industries, including charcoal-burning for iron smelting.

Tudor and Stuart England

Though by this time the village pattern had been laid down, and few or no new settlements were made at the expense of forested land, two uses for timber must have made great inroads on the numbers of standing trees. One was the need for timber for wooden ships, and the other was to produce yet more charcoal for the smelting of iron ore. So profound was the effect of the latter process, that by 1565 it was found necessary to suppress all the bloomeries in Furness, in order that the woods might be no further destroyed. In the mid-seventeenth century this restriction was lifted, and soon the English woods were so devastated that the chief ironmasters transferred their works to the Scottish Highlands, where some of them began the destruction of the oak forests on the sides of Loch Maree and at other places.

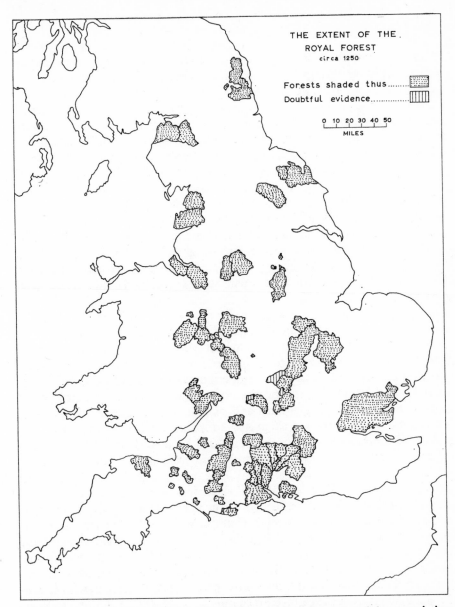

Figure 24. English Forests remaining by 1250 A.D. Reproduced by permission of the Cambridge University Press, from "Historical Geography of England before 1800" by H. C. Darby (after N. L. Beazley, Transactions of the Royal Historical Society).

Scotland and Ireland

From Scotland, there is as yet comparatively little detailed evidence on vegetation history during the historic period, apart from that shown in Fig. 20—Turner's evidence from Perthshire and Ayrshire. There is, as Turner points out (1965), little evidence for much Iron Age agricultural activity in Scotland, and it is in agreement with this that there are no signs of extensive clearance in her pollen diagrams from Scotland until the latter part of Roman times. Recent work just south of the Border, in Weardale and the Lake District, has emphasised the importance of this late Romano-British agricultural activity. These episodes of extensive clearance in Perthshire and Ayrshire were, however, only temporary; this is in complete contrast with the history at Tregaron. In Scotland the woodland subsequently regenerated, and it was not until recent centuries that complete clearance occurred—see Fig. 20. It is well known from historical sources that the great Caledonian forest persisted for long after the more southerly parts of Britain were cleared and settled, and the history of the Scottish forests will be discussed more fully in the next chapter.

Mitchell's pollen diagram which he gives as typical of Ireland is shown in Fig. 21. The main change in agricultural history in this country dates from about 300 A.D., and this is the time which Mitchell considered to mark the introduction of more advanced agricultural techniques, including ox-drawn ploughs, into Ireland. The Christian period had begun in Ireland before the arrival of St Patrick in 431, and the accounts of the early Christian period include mention of plough-teams and plough-shares. The Celtic monastic movement began in Ireland about 500 A.D., and Mitchell believes that agricultural development was further stimulated by this. Later episodes which he correlates with the history of Ireland are a period of woodland regeneration which could well show the results of Viking destruction of many of the monasteries, and then further agricultural extensions which could correlate with the English invasions and settlement. The corpse of a man dressed in garments of the fifteenth or sixteenth century, which was recovered from the peat of an Irish bog, showed that he had been eating rye grain in which the corn-cockle (*Agrostemma githago*) had been a weed. The Tudor conquest of Ireland led to further exploitation of the woodlands for timber, with accelerated forest clearance. Then followed the period of Afforestation, which, as in England, dates from the eighteenth century.

Enclosures

One typically British habitat, the hedgerow, which is in the artificial or man-made group, includes several different types, of different ages. As Salisbury points out, many ancient and broad hedges probably represent surviving narrow belts of woodland, which were never completely cleared, but were left as windbreaks and boundaries between pastures and between cultivated fields. In some parts of the country the field boundaries are of great antiquity, but in others, particularly in the areas of dense Anglo-Saxon settlement, the great open fields of the mediaeval villages were enclosed at various times in the sixteenth and seventeenth, and to the biggest extent of all in the eighteenth, centuries. Some villages retained their open fields into the early nineteenth century. When the enclosure took place, miles of new hedges had to be planted to fence the enclosed ground. In all types of hedge, trees and shrubs and many herbs of the natural habitat of the woodland margin now find a suitable habitat. Various species of elm, and the ash are now very characteristic hedgerow trees; in many parts of England, such as the Midlands, the hedgerow trees give an exaggerated impression of the degree to which the countryside is afforested. Of the shrubs which in prehistoric times found their habitat on woodland margins and the edges of clearings, two thorns, the hawthorn (*Crataegus monogyna*) and the Blackthorn (*Prunus spinosa*) have become hedgeformers, with many other shrubs, like the Guelder Rose (*Viburnum opulus*), and in calcareous districts the Privet (*Ligustrum vulgare*) and the Buckthorn (*Rhamnus catharticus*). Among characteristic hedgerow herbs, those from the natural flora of woodland margins or scrub include Cow-parsley (*Anthriscus sylvestris*), Hedge-parsley (*Torilis japonica*) and Jack-by-the-hedge (*Alliaria petiolata*).

In his recent book on "Fieldwork in Local History", Professor Hoskins discusses English hedge-banks of different dates,—"ranging all the way from the second century to the nineteenth"—and presents interesting evidence obtained by himself and Dr Max Hooper in support of their theory that the older the hedge-bank, the greater is the number of shrub species present in it.

Forestry

During the eighteenth century many landlords began to conserve and extend existing woodlands on their estates, by enclosure to exclude grazing animals, and by planting. This planting included individuals of the still surviving native trees, such as oaks and ash, but also beech in the areas (such as northern England, Ireland and Scotland) where it had been naturally either absent or very rare, and the pine (*Pinus sylvestris*) which may by that time have been extinct in England, Wales and Ireland. In all these countries, many pollen diagrams show a phase, very near the top, which is distinguished by appreciable amounts of *Pinus* and *Fagus* pollen, and is called by Mitchell in Ireland the Afforestation period. The sycamore (*Acer pseudo-platanus*), a tree which had been widely introduced in the fifteenth or sixteenth century, was planted extensively in the late sixteenth and early seventeenth century. In the absence of heavy grazing it regenerates very readily in most parts of Britain, and the increased care of amenity woodlands in the eighteenth century encouraged the growth and spread of sycamore. The European Larch (*Larix decidua*), a tree of the Alpine region of Europe, first introduced in the seventeenth century, is another alien which regenerates freely, under British conditions, and often appears, as in the Lake District, to be growing in the manner of a native tree. Another conifer introduced at about the same time was the silver fir, *Abies alba*.

The extension of planted woodlands including beech, pine, larch, fir and sycamore proceeded through the nineteenth century on private estates. After the great increase in demand for home-grown timber during the First World War, the afforestation of marginal agricultural land began, and the Forestry Commission acquired land for state forests, mainly in the treeless uplands, but also in lowland areas of poor soil like the Breckland. The native deciduous trees are on the whole too demanding as regards soil to flourish now in such habitats, so alien conifers, which can make good growth in poorer soils and under cool oceanic conditions, have been used. Of these, the Norway spruce (*Picea abies*), another alien which was first introduced in the sixteenth century, was very widely planted; this is one of the most important of the soft-wood timber trees, and thinnings from the plantations supply the Christmas trees every year. Other important timber trees now widely planted in Britain are the Sitka spruce (*Picea sitchensis*) and the Lodgepole Pine (*Pinus contorta*), both natives of the western coastal parts of North America. These two trees do particularly well on the upland Forestry Commission lands of the northern and western hills. With *Picea abies*, they make up the blanket of dark alien conifers which, particularly when planted in unrelieved straight lines, are so much resented by many lovers of the landscape of the hills of Wales, northern England and southern Scotland. In the Scottish Highlands afforestation has been more extensively with the native Scots Pine which flourishes very well there, and has therefore changed the character of the landscape less.

10

British vegetation history I. Dry land vegetation-forests, grasslands, heaths and coastal habitats

THIS chapter and the next will give short accounts of what is known of the history of certain particularly interesting kinds of vegetation in Britain, but can only describe the vegetation very briefly. Anyone interested in British vegetation must consult Tansley's classic work "The British Islands and their Vegetation", which gives an unrivalled account of the physical environment, the nature and classification of vegetation types in Britain. The vegetation of Scotland is described and comprehensively analysed by other methods—those of the phytosociologist—in "The Vegetation of Scotland", edited by Burnett. Pearsall's "Mountains and Moorlands" presents an account of all aspects of the ecology of the Highland zone of Britain, emphasising the dynamic concept of changing soils and vegetation during the Post-glacial period. This section of the present small book can be no more than an introduction to the subject of historical ecology, and anyone interested is urged to pursue it in one of these larger works, and especially in the recently published revision, by Dr M. C. F. Proctor, of Tansley's shorter book "Britain's Green Mantle".

Forests

In Tansley's analysis of "The nature and status of British Woodlands"—Chapter XII in "The British Islands and their Vegetation", the following trees are listed as dominant in British woodlands:

Quercus robur—Pedunculate oak
Quercus petraea—Sessile oak
Fagus sylvatica—Beech
Betula pendula ⎱Birch
Betula pubescens ⎰

Fraxinus excelsior—Ash
Pinus sylvestris—Pine
Alnus glutinosa—Alder

and as "other trees" Tansley cites:

Taxus baccata—Yew
Carpinus betulus—Hornbeam
Ilex aquifolium—Holly
Acer pseudo-platanus—Sycamore
Acer campestre—Maple
Ulmus glabra—Wych elm
Salix species—Willows
Sorbus aucuparia—Rowan

Sorbus aria—Whitebeam
Pyrus malus (*Malus sylvestris*)—Crab apple
Prunus avium—Cherry or Gean
Prunus padus—Bird Cherry
Tilia cordata—Small-leaved lime
Tilia platyphyllos—Large-leaved lime
Populus species—Poplars

and among the "more important shrubs" according to Tansley, are:

Corylus avellana—Hazel
Crataegus monogyna—Hawthorn

Juniperus communis—Juniper
Other species of *Salix*—Willows

As a result of the researches described in the earlier part of this book, it is now known that of this list, pine and the birches have been forest-formers in Britain since the end of the Late-glacial period, more than 9000 years ago, and that juniper and the aspen (*Populus tremula*) and several species of willows have been in Britain since Late-glacial times. Among the early immigrant species after the beginning of the Post-glacial were the hazel, the Wych elm and the oaks; later came the alder, the small-leaved lime (*Tilia cordata*), ash and holly, and later still, beech and hornbeam. Lime, beech and hornbeam did not reach Ireland. *Acer campestre*, which does not seem to be native in Scotland or Ireland, was first recorded from England in Neolithic times, and the sycamore, *Acer pseudo-platanus*, was introduced in the fifteenth or sixteenth century and regenerates freely. *Taxus baccata*, yew, has not been regularly recognised in pollen analysis, but macroscopic records of it date from the Boreal period. The history of the trees and shrubs of the family Rosaceae is still incompletely known, because only the most recent refinements in pollen recognition can separate the species of *Sorbus*, *Pyrus* and *Prunus* on pollen morphology. Macroscopic remains of the trees of these genera are known from the second half of the Post-glacial, but it seems likely that further refinements in pollen recognition will show that they were present in Britain in earlier periods.

The present distribution of the British trees is the result of integrations of many complex factors, and these are examined in Tansley's account. He recognises as types of native British woodlands today: Oakwoods, including Pedunculate oakwoods and Sessile oakwoods, Beechwoods, Ashwoods, Pinewoods and Birchwoods—the two last being found only in Scotland. The history of each type will be considered in turn.

Oakwoods

Quercus robur, the Pedunculate oak, and *Quercus petraea*, the Sessile oak, tend to grow on different soils, with *Q. robur* on heavy clay soils, mainly in lowland places, and *Q. petraea* on lighter and thinner soils in the uplands, but since hybrids form readily between them, it is not possible to make a complete separation. The pollen of the two species is indistinguishable, so in considering the evidence on the history of oakwoods which is derived from pollen analysis, the two types of oakwood must be taken together. Oakwood with a proportion of other trees, and characteristic shrubs and "ground flora" of herbs, constitutes the "climatic climax" vegetation of that part of Britain which is not wet enough for the formation of peat, nor so high in altitude or latitude that birch or pine becomes the climax tree. In this part of Britain, oaks grow well and produce good crops of acorns, which can germinate to produce new trees, but very frequently nowadays do not do so. This is either because the acorns are all eaten by small animals such as voles and mice, or if the acorns survive and grow into seedlings, these are in so many woods nibbled by rabbits, sheep or deer until the growing point is destroyed and the seedling dies.

The history of a lowland oakwood in the southern Lake District is illustrated by Fig. 22, which shows the pollen diagram from Blelham Tarn; the tarn and its immediate surroundings are shown in the air photograph in Plate 3. The surviving areas of woodland can be seen in the air photograph, and compared with the somewhat greater area which is pasture or arable fields. In the surface mud from the middle of the tarn, tree pollen makes up 40 per cent of the total pollen, and this is a figure within the usually accepted limits for a partially deforested landscape. From the horizon of the Boreal/Atlantic transition, the zone boundary VIc/VIIa, the alder has contributed a very steady proportion of the total tree pollen. The alder is here found in wet places and along streams, and the dry land forest has been predominantly of oak until the second of the major episodes of forest clearance; since this time, birch has become of equal importance with the oak. The Atlantic period of primary forest without any herbaceous pollen ended with the Elm Decline, after which ash appeared and elm remained very scarce, and in this secondary forest, herbs such as *Mercurialis* appeared in the pollen spectrum. After the long period of secondary forest, three separate episodes of forest clearance and partial regeneration can be seen in the pollen diagram. The first has the character of a Landnam or "small temporary clearance", the second shows a steep diminution in oak and expansion of grass and herbs of grassland, leading on to regeneration of the pioneer tree, birch, and only partial replacement of this by oak, and the third, with a prolonged increase in grass pollen and decrease in that of oak, with the first appearance of cereals, and of many weeds, indicates the most prolonged and permanent of the attacks on the oakwood. The surviving oakwood seems to have remained at about the same extent after this, and at the top of the diagram the reappearance of pine and the appearance of beech must mark the beginning of the Afforestation period, while at the same time the increase in birch at the expense of alder probably shows the effects of drainage of some of the swampy land. Holly (*Ilex*) first appeared in the pollen spectrum with the initial Landnam clearance and thereafter shows a continuous curve; this is most probably explained by the power of this shrub to survive grazing. The oakwood has probably been grazed, at least periodically, ever since the Landnam clearance.

There are two well-known high-altitude oakwoods on acid soil, which have every appearance of being natural, and very probably represent surviving vestiges of the type of upland oakwood which formerly flourished at altitudes of up to about 2500 feet, before the Bronze Age upland settlements began. Wistman's Wood, Plate 11, between 1200 and 1400 feet up on Dartmoor, is of *Quercus robur*, and the Keskadale Oaks in the Lake District, of *Quercus petraea*, lie between 1000 and 1500 feet. Both woods seem to owe their survival to the nature of the ground, which has discouraged grazing animals. In the Dartmoor wood the ground is of granite boulders, and in the Keskadale Oaks it is a stony stabilised scree on a slope of about 40 degrees. The oaks in both woods seem liable to parasitic attack by fungi and gall flies, and Tansley considers that the altitude of these woods, that is, about 1500 feet, is now "really limiting to oaks in the climate of western England". This is therefore evidence that our present climate is less favourable to tree growth than that of the Atlantic and possibly Sub-Boreal periods, and that the present upper limit for oaks is about a thousand feet lower than it was in 3000 B.C. In both these high-level oakwoods, the only other tree is the rowan, *Sorbus aucuparia*: both it and the oaks appear to be producing seedlings. *Vaccinium myrtillus*, the bilberry, is common to the ground flora of both woods, and the bracken (*Pteridium aquilinum*) grows in gaps between the trees where light reaches the ground.

Beechwoods

Beech woodland, as now found on calcareous soils in south-eastern England— the Chiltern hills, parts of the North and South Downs, and the Cotswolds, is a very characteristic vegetation type, but seems to be comparatively recent in origin. In British pollen diagrams, *Fagus* pollen is only found in quantity in Godwin's Zone VIII—that is, from about 500 B.C. onwards, and this only in south-eastern England. It may be that our record for *Fagus* is still incomplete, because there are so few pollen diagrams from the chalk and oolitic limestone country, which is now the beechwood country, but from existing diagrams it seems that *Fagus* was not common in Britain until the Sub-Atlantic period, though it had been present in parts, such as Hampshire, since Atlantic times. There are records of wood and charcoal of beech from Neolithic times onward, so the native status of beech is proved beyond question, but it is difficult to explain why it should have expanded during Zone VIII, the Sub-Atlantic period, *after* the climatic deterioration at the opening of the Sub-

Atlantic. This expansion of the beech is found at the same time in pollen diagrams from Denmark and North Germany. The beech today seems to be climatically limited from spreading, as a forest tree, to north and west of the present area of natural beechwoods, by late spring frosts, low summer temperatures, and soil degeneration in the areas of high rainfall. Planted beech trees in the north and west, however, can often be seen to be producing seedlings, which seem to succumb mainly to grazing. Godwin has suggested that an anthropogenic factor may be involved, in that the calcareous, well-drained soils now occupied by the beech were almost certainly extensively deforested by prehistoric settlement up to Romano-British times, and if, as seems likely, human pressure on the upland chalk and limestone areas was relaxed as metal axes and heavier ploughs made it possible to clear and cultivate the clay soils, then the beech may have been able to colonise rapidly the abandoned lands, though for many previous millennia it had been unable to penetrate into closed mixed-oak forest. This would explain the expansion of beech pollen which begins with the beginning of the Iron Age.

Ashwoods

Ashwoods form another woodland type which is characteristic of calcareous soils, here particularly the Carboniferous limestone of the Mendips and northern England, and the Durness Limestone of Scotland. The pollen record, from such sites as Malham Tarn, suggests that these pure ashwoods are of no greater antiquity than the beechwoods, though at most sites ash has a more continuous representation in pollen diagrams throughout the Sub-Boreal period. Both ash and beech tend to be under-represented in the pollen rain, so it is as yet difficult to assess their true contribution to the primary forest of Britain, but there is no doubt that their relative importance has increased since anthropogenic forest clearance became widespread. *Fraxinus*, the ash, would seem to have had two main periods of expansion into British woodlands—the first, at the Elm Decline, when thinning of the primary forest provided the opportunity for the ash to penetrate into what had formerly been a closed canopy of oak–elm–birch or oak–elm–lime, and the second, much later, when widespread forest clearance (and abandonment of cleared patches) had provided new habitats for recolonisation by trees. Under present conditions, on neutral or calcareous soils, ash regenerates readily wherever its seedlings can obtain sufficient light, and it would seem to be well adapted to the role of a secondary forest-former, on suitable soils.

Pine and birchwoods

Native pine forest is today found only in the Scottish Highlands, where in Rothiemurchus, the Black Wood of Rannoch, and in many smaller woodlands, such as those of upper Glen Affric and Coille na Glas Leitire on Beinn Eighe, naturally grown and usually regenerating pine has every appearance of being a primary forest former. Such evidence as exists from pollen analysis at Highland sites confirms that these areas represent the few remaining survivals of primary pine forest which has been the climax vegetation of those parts since Boreal times. "Natural" reduction in the area of pine forest was brought about by the development of blanket peat in the highly oceanic climate of the North-west Highlands, and abundant remains of pine trunks and stumps in blanket peat testify to the former presence of pine forest in areas now totally deforested and peat-covered. The earliest records of undoubtedly anthropogenic forest clearance in the north-west have been dated by radiocarbon to the later part of the chambered cairns period (2700–1300 B.C.). No botanical evidence is yet available to confirm the historical theory that widespread forest destruction by fire accompanied the Scandinavian settlements of 800–1100 A.D. but many as yet undated charcoal layers are present in the peat. In the later eighteenth and early nineteenth centuries came the development of sheep-farming in the Highlands, which pushed the crofters to the coastal fringes and greatly accelerated the decline of the native forests of both pine and birch. Not only was much forest felled to provide further grazing, but in the surviving forests the regeneration of trees was drastically reduced wherever the sheep were allowed to graze. Finally there came the demands for timber of two World Wars, and by then the former ancient forest of Caledon originally described by Tacitus was reduced to isolated remnants. In the woods which remain, it is not always clear what factors govern the separation of birch and pine, but the areas of predominantly birch forest are now in the far north, Caithness and Sutherland, and on the western coasts of the mainland and in the islands, while pine is the dominant tree of the central and eastern Highlands. If pine forest is felled or burned, birch is the tree which regenerates in it. Being a short-lived tree, birch forms woods which are not permanent; many Highland birchwoods at present consist of trees of similar age which are now almost moribund, but in other areas, saplings which will form the woods of the future are thick on the ground. Grazing is one factor which determines whether regeneration will take place, in most woods, but burning of heather moors is another potent factor in preventing regeneration of trees. Even the surviving fragments of Highland birch forest on islands in lochs, which often present such a contrast to the burned and grazed heather moors around them, will often be found to have been extensively, if seasonally, grazed by sheep during times of population pressure in the Highlands, and so will differ in their shrub layer and ground flora from truly primary forest. In addition, many island woods are significantly affected by the browsing of red deer. A good example, a birch-rowan wood, is found on Eilean Mor in Loch Sionascaig, in the Inverpolly Nature Reserve, and shown in Plate 6.

Shrubs

Shrubs, which in places now form characteristic vegetation types, must have been restricted before 3000 B.C. to those which can flourish under the canopy of deciduous woodland. Hawthorn (*Crataegus* sp.), Guelder Rose (*Viburnum opulus*) and dogwood (*Cornus sanguinea*), together with holly and ivy, have been recorded from Boreal times onwards as part of the primary forest flora. Most shrubs would find new habitats with the extension of the forest margin which accompanied clearance, and when grasslands were established, changes in population pressure would provide new habitats for shrubs as part of the seral succession back to forest when cleared land was abandoned. This process can be seen today on chalk grassland where sheep are no longer grazed and where rabbit pressure has been reduced; the grassland is soon colonised by hawthorn seedlings or by juniper, and eventually beechwood results. Other shrubs associated with hawthorn and juniper are dogwood, privet, and buckthorn (*Rhamnus catharticus*) on calcareous soils. On other soils, hawthorn, blackthorn (*Prunus spinosa*) and elder (*Sambucus nigra*) are common as colonisers of land where cultivation or grazing pressure is relaxed.

Juniper (*Juniperus communis*) is now known from several other distinctive plant communities, of which the history has probably been very different. High-level juniper scrub above the present tree-line may represent its survival through the Post-glacial forest period, outside the climatic limits of tolerance of trees—thus the prostrate juniper scrub above the present tree-line on Beinn Eighe may be the closest existing approach to the juniper community of the Late-glacial period. Other juniper communities in northern England seem to represent a stage in woodland degeneration, where this is due to felling or grazing. Juniper does not flourish where the soil is leached and acid, as a rule, but can be found on peat.

Grasslands and heaths

It has been shown how the techniques of Quaternary Research have produced evidence for the anthropogenic origin of all British grassland except the high-montane type.

High montane grassland

This, in Pearsall's view, constitutes a natural development from the *Rhacomitrium* heath which colonises bare mountain-top detritus. *Rhacomitrium lanuginosum*, the woolly hair moss, plus a number of lichens, seem to be the first colonisers, and humus-formers, on newly-stabilised rock-waste or scree, and in the stable carpet so developed grasses such as *Festuca ovina* (Sheep's fescue), *Deschampsia flexuosa* (Wavy Hair-grass) and *Agrostis tenuis* (Bent) are among the first of flowering plants to gain a foothold. The constancy of many of the allied species in this vegetation type shows a quite striking relationship with what appear to have been common Late-glacial plant communities, though unfortunately it is not as yet possible to distinguish the species of grasses on their pollen morphology. Such plants as *Galium saxatile* (Heath Bedstraw), *Vaccinium* (Bilberry), *Empetrum* (Crowberry), *Salix herbacea* (Least willow) and the two common club-mosses, *Lycopodium selago* and *L. clavatum,* commonly now associated with high-level grassland, are among those most commonly found associated with high frequencies of grass and sedge pollen in Late-glacial pollen spectra, at least in Highland Britain. In both instances, this represents a plant community capable of active colonisation of skeletal soils and of surviving conditions unfavourable to the growth of trees. Many variations of high-montane grassland can be found in Britain, on rocks of different composition, but sheep-grazing, where at all heavy, has tended to suppress the more interesting species and encourage the growth of the unpalatable mat-grass (*Nardus stricta*).

Breckland

This wide treeless area of grass-heath and richer grasslands has already been mentioned in Chapter 7 as an area of special interest to ecologists, and one now shown to have been originally deforested in Neolithic times. Various environmental factors, such as the prevailingly sandy nature of the soil, the rather low rainfall, and the very heavy grazing by rabbits, which were formerly thought to have been the cause of the treelessness of Breckland, are now seen rather as the factors which helped to keep open the vegetation after the primary destruction of the trees by Neolithic men. The grasslands on the less acid soils of comparatively high base-status contain a rich variety of species, including a few which are now found only here in Britain, and have a steppe distribution in Europe. Among these are *Silene otites, Veronica triphyllos,* and *Artemisia campestris.*

The vegetation of Upper Teesdale

The botanically famous area of Upper Teesdale includes vegetation types which are probably best considered with the grasslands, though of a very special type. Like the high-montane grasslands just discussed, the Upper Teesdale plant communities represent a vegetation which is closely related to that of the Late-glacial period. All the existing evidence agrees in indicating that parts of this area must have remained in general a refuge, free of trees, all through the Post-glacial forest period. As a result, its plants present a record of the flora and vegetation of Late-glacial Britain which is unique and irreplaceable. Many of the characteristic plants of Upper Teesdale are rare, and many are beautiful by any criterion, but it is neither the beauty nor the rarity which is the primary cause of the concern which botanists have for this area—its most important feature is the continued existence of communities which must resemble those which covered most of Britain during the five millennia while the last great ice-cap was retreating into the mountains and finally disappearing.

The factors which have preserved these communities resembling those of the Late-glacial in Upper Teesdale are even now not completely understood. The relatively high humidity and low mean temperature, resulting from the altitude, are certainly important, and equally so is the composition of the rock. "Teesdale possesses a character of its own, which is constituted of the features associated with the Great Whin Sill and the sugar limestone, the high limestone scars and the extensive spread of calcareous boulder clay, in an area where the overall combination of altitude and climate is peculiarly favourable to the northern and Sub-alpine nature of the vegetation" (Pigott, 1956). Pigott has shown that around the floristically famous grassland areas, remains of former forest are abundant under the blanket peat, and considers that the high level limestone scars were probably a most important refuge through the Post-glacial forest period for many of the Teesdale plants which require unshaded, base-rich soils. He visualises the present level limestone outcrops as probably covered with thin forest or with a scrub of *Corylus* and *Juniperus* during Atlantic time, and points out that some of the rare plants could have survived under such conditions—*Viola rupestris*, *Carex ericetorum* and *Dryas octopetala* under light scrub, and *Gentiana verna* and *Polygala amara* in openings of the tree canopy. The craggy limestone scars and areas where the streams have been continually eroding calcareous moraines must however have remained as open habitats throughout the Post-glacial period (and so must the riverside habitats where *Potentilla fruticosa* is now found) and in addition there is the particular liability to wind erosion of the soils derived from the sugar limestone—the chemically altered limestone produced by the heat of the intrusion into the Carboniferous limestone of the dolerite of the Great Whin Sill. At this altitude, up to 1500 feet, wind force may have been strong enough to keep at least some of these soils too unstable to allow the development of a continuous woodland cover. On steep slopes, at this altitude, winter solifluction increases the instability of the soils. All these factors may well have contributed to the preservation in the area of open habitats in which shade-intolerant plants were able to live through the Post-glacial forest period.

Pigott and others have described several different types of grassland communities. Meadows now used for hay and only very lightly grazed, in autumn, at the high farms such as Birkdale, show a rich variety of herbs, very different from the rather dull hill grassland which is common in northern England. These meadows are derived, Pigott considers, from the field layer of a herb-rich birch woodland, containing also *Prunus padus*, the Bird Cherry. The herbs, many of which have been recorded from the Late-glacial period, include *Crepis paludosa*, *Cirsium heterophyllum*, *Valeriana dioica*, and *Filipendula ulmaria*, with *Geranium sylvaticum*, *Trollius europaeus*, *Caltha palustris*, *Alchemilla glabra* and *Achillea ptarmica*. The long growing season which is necessary for the hay crop at this altitude has preserved these meadows from intensive grazing, and the soils are good brown earths, flushed with calcareous water. The remaining fragments of this type of herb-rich birchwood in the area may well represent the nearest present-day equivalent to the Allerød birchwoods of northern England.

In wetter places, this type of meadow gives way to a closed turf of the Purple Moor Grass (*Molinia caerulea*), with *Trollius* and *Geranium sylvaticum* if cattle are excluded. In the turf occur occasionally the rarer plants, *Gentiana verna*, *Bartsia alpina*, and *Primula farinosa*. When cattle are allowed into such a grassland, their trampling, on this particular soil type, produces a fragmentation of the turf into isolated hummocks which were probably initiated by frost action, and then exposure of limestone gravel as the organic soil is worn away. Many of the rare plants of Teesdale are found on these hummocks and on the gravel irrigated with calcareous water—these include *Tofieldia pusilla* (Scottish Asphodel), *Carex capillaris*, *Juncus alpinus*, *Kobresia simpliciuscula*, and *Saxifraga aizoides*, as well as *Primula farinosa* (Bird's Eye Primrose) and *Bartsia alpina*. Where considerable areas of sugar limestone gravel, irrigated by calcareous water, are found, the scattered individual plants include the rare *Minuartia stricta* (Plate 26), as well as *Minuartia verna*, and two plants now normally found on the coasts—*Armeria maritima* (Thrift) and *Plantago maritima* (Sea plantain); these too are commonly recorded from the Late-glacial flora.

Another type of turf, found on weathered sugar limestone where wind erosion is active, includes *Dryas octopetala* (Mountain avens), and also the Rock-roses, *Helianthemum canum* and *H. chamaecistus*, as well as *Viola rupestris*, *Carex ericetorum*, *Thymus drucei*, *Carex capillaris*, *Thalictrum alpinum*, and *Polygala amara*. This is perhaps one of the most characteristic Teesdale habitats.

On ordinary unaltered Carboniferous limestone, the grassland turf, made up of the grasses *Sesleria*, *Festuca* and *Koeleria*, contains *Gentiana verna* and another rarity, *Myosotis alpestris*, as well as *Minuartia verna* and *Thymus drucei*. Pigott believes that this type of limestone grassland is perpetuated in its present form by heavy grazing by sheep and rabbits.

After this Teesdale plant assemblage had been recognised for so long as a relict of the Late-glacial vegetation, it was of enormous interest when *Betula nana*, one of the most characteristic of Late-glacial plants, was recently discovered in one of the areas of peaty soil. It seems very possible that this is another relict (comparable with this plant's station on Lüenberg Heath in

Germany), where remains of the plant may well eventually be found to trace the continuity all through the Post-glacial period from Late-glacial times.

The Burren, Co Clare

This striking district where the Carboniferous limestone outcrops in horizontal beds at sea level, in a climate so extremely oceanic that wet humus accumulates on the surface of the limestone, carries a vegetation unlike that found anywhere else in Britain. This seems to arise from the combination of low summer temperatures and bedrock of high base-status. The limestone surface (which in a drier climate would be bare, carrying only scanty drought-resisting plants), here develops a thin humus on which develops a turf of *Festuca ovina*, *Sesleria caerulea* and *Koeleria cristata*, with abundant *Dryas octopetala* and other herbs which prefer calcareous soils. But owing to accumulation of pockets of acid humus, among this lime-loving vegetation grow calcifuge (lime-hating) plants such as *Calluna* and *Empetrum nigrum*, whose natural habitat is acid heath. On the Burren limestone are found also other plants which are normally mountain species, like *Dryas octopetala*—these are *Arenaria norvegica* and *Saxifraga hypnoides*. The vegetation of the Burren is fully described in two of the New Naturalist books—Mountain Flowers, and Flowers of the Chalk and Limestone, and by Ivimey-Cook and Proctor (1966).

Heath and moors

This term in general means a vegetation dominated by the ling (*Calluna vulgaris*). Lowland heaths are usually found on areas of light sandy soils, unrewarding in cultivation, such as the Tertiary sands of the London and Hampshire Basins, and the Greensand formation as seen at Hindhead and other places in Surrey. Upland heaths are generally known as heather moors, and these pass into upland Callunetum on wet shallow peat which is transitional to blanket bog. Over great areas of north-west Europe, Callunetum has replaced trees, on soils where factors were present which prevented regeneration of trees after prehistoric forest clearance. The state of the soil in some of these woodlands has been described by Pigott: "Under deciduous woodland containing oak, holly and hazel, an acid brown-earth is developed in which there is little evidence of podsolisation, but removal of the tree canopy or even grazing of the field layer can initiate changes which allow a rapid development of a podsol. All the evidence suggests that these acid brown-earths are in a delicately balanced equilibrium, and much of the nutrient capital of the soil is continuously circulated by the vegetation and soil fauna. Any interruption of this circulation has disastrous consequences". After felling of the trees, such soils became rapidly podsolised and most of them have remained as heaths ever since, except where large-scale agricultural works have been started to reclaim them for cultivation. This happened in Jutland in the late nineteenth century (under the stimulus of the loss of so much land to Prussia), and has continued until the present day. One factor potent in keeping open the vegetation of many heaths has been the repeated burning to which many of them have been subjected, destroying any tree seedlings. *Calluna* moors where grouse or sheep feed are deliberately fired (moor-burn) in order to reduce the amount of old dead wood in the bushes and induce them to put out new shoots, which are palatable and nutritious. Lowland heaths must have been similarly treated in the interests of sheep-grazing, and of course accidental fires have contributed to the destruction of any trees (usually pine or birch) which might have colonised them. *Calluna* does not, however, stand up well to heavy grazing, and either overstocking with sheep, or a large rabbit population, will quickly convert heath to grass-land. Stages in the establishment of a *Nardus* grassland, where burning has led to bare areas of soil, have been described. *Calluna*, which is a calcifuge species, grows well on soils of low base-status, and can tolerate a high degree of acidity. It is a plant of oceanic and sub-oceanic climatic regimes, and in areas of high rainfall it can become established even in the thin leached surface layer of a limestone soil.

Several aspects of the history of Callunetum have been investigated. Andersen's work on the interglacial lake sediments in Denmark has shown that a changeover from forest to heath occurred on sandy soils during the closing stages of the last (the Ipswichian) interglacial period, and so this must be regarded as, to some extent at least, a natural and not an entirely anthropo-genic process. In the Ipswichian Interglacial, the process must have taken place under purely natural conditions, though perhaps accelerated by forest fires caused by lightning.

Calluna is characteristically a plant of podsols, and this soil profile develops very rapidly on sandy soils. Leaching by rainwater is active in all free-draining soils, but the highly leached mineral horizon of a podsol is produced by the passage of rainwater containing dissolved organic acids from the layer of undecomposed and only partially decomposed plant remains which forms the surface layer. The litter or surface layer produced by the remains of *Calluna* plants gives rise to a highly acid raw humus, so the process of pod-solisation is accelerated when *Calluna* forms the dominant vegetation.

Calluna moors are very well developed in the Cleveland Hills of north-east Yorkshire. Erdtman carried out a number of pollen analyses on peat-bog profiles in this region, to find out whether this vegetation type is primary or secondary, and found that for the early part of the Post-glacial period, forest history had followed a similar course here to that in the rest of the country. Dimbleby has extended this work by investigating soil pollen in the area, and has found that the old soil surfaces which were buried under Bronze Age barrows contain much pollen of deciduous woodland, in complete contrast to the present soils outside the barrows, because these contain pollen over-whelmingly dominated by *Calluna*. His conclusion is that during the Bronze Age, the area must have been forested, and that the origin of the Callunetum dates from Bronze Age deforestation. The composition of the pollen spectrum from within the barrows indicates a type of woodland which would only flourish on a good brown-earth soil, whereas the soil outside the barrows is now strongly podsolised. Dimbleby interprets this as evidence that the pod-solisation of the soils of this area dates from the change over from deciduous forest to Callunetum.

Upland *Calluna* moor is of course found very extensively in Scotland now. Work by McVean and others on the Scottish pine forests suggests that pine would be capable of colonising much of this Callunetum if burning did not take place, and if a great variety of animals which either eat the seeds or graze on the young seedlings were excluded: these animals range from slugs and beetles through rodents and birds to sheep and red deer. Probably most of the Scottish heather moors originally bore pine or birch forest; over wide areas pine would perhaps have been able to regenerate after prehistoric fires, naturally or anthropogenically caused, had it not been for the local abundance of one or more of these destructive animals. It may well be that under natural conditions, *Calluna* moor (primary Callunetum) was restricted to the wind-swept ridges.

The Pennine "moors" occupy the areas of pronounced slope and moderate rainfall; where the slope is less, or the rainfall more than about 45 in., the layer of *mor* humus on the podsol profile increases in depth and becomes peat, and the vegetation changes to that of damp moorland, with cotton-sedge (*Eriophorum*) and *Sphagnum*, and so to blanket bog. The Pennine heather moors have clearly been derived from upland oakwood or birchwood, and are maintained in their present state by regular burning.

Coastal habitats

In considering the question of where the light-demanding, shade-intolerant species, and those unable to succeed in closed plant communities, could have survived from the Late-glacial vegetation through the forest period of the mid-Post-glacial, we have seen that two possible refuges were available. Plants which could tolerate sub-Arctic climatic conditions at high altitudes were able to survive, as in Upper Teesdale, on high crags and high montane grasslands. The continuity of such species in the flora has been proved by pollen analysis of the lake sediments of Llyn Idwal in its high corrie in Snow-donia. Other plants, which can tolerate maritime conditions of severe exposure and salt spray, found congenial habitats on coastal shingle banks and sand dunes, where the wind force and shifting nature of the substratum prevented the growth of trees.

One small group of plants was able to survive in both habitats. Two of the commonest of seaside plants, *Armeria maritima* and *Plantago maritima*, both common in the Late-glacial flora at most sites investigated, have already been cited as members of the Teesdale flora, and are found also in many other mountain stations; both are present through the Post-glacial deposits in Cwm Idwal. It seems that both plants, in their present coastal and inland mountain habitats, represent remains of a much more continuously distributed population in Late-glacial times. *Armeria maritima* is a variable plant, and some authorities have distinguished a species *A. vulgaris*, with varieties *maritima* and *alpina* for the coastal and mountain populations respectively. Baker, after extensive work, regards all British *Armerias* as forming a single species, *A. maritima* Willd., and this agrees with the conception of the present coastal and mountain populations as remnants of a single widely dispersed Late-glacial population.

A vegetation type characteristic of extremely exposed situations on the west coasts of Ireland and the Hebridean islands is dominated by *Plantago maritima*, forming a close sward. With it grow *Plantago coronopus* and various grasses, including *Aira praecox* and *Festuca ovina*. Investigation of the peat found below this vegetation on St Kilda suggests that this community is of considerable antiquity.

Another maritime plant commonly recorded in Late-glacial deposits is *Hippophae rhamnoides*, the Sea Buckthorn. This is now a shrub of calcareous dunes on the east coast of England. In the Late-glacial period it seems to have found a congenial habitat on unstable, unleached glacial sands and gravels, but apparently it was unable to withstand competition by trees, and so died out in Britain from all except its coastal habitats. On the Continent it is also found on the shingle banks of mountain streams.

Species of many shade-intolerant genera such as *Rumex*, *Polygonum*, *Chenopodium*, *Artemisia*, *Matricaria* and *Silene*, are common in the vegetation of coastal sand and shingle and estuarine silt. Pollen morphology is as yet of only limited use in the determination of species of these genera, so it has not been possible to demonstrate the continuity of these coastal populations with the Late-glacial vegetation, but it may well be that the species which are now such common weeds of cultivated land were able to survive from the Late-glacial vegetation in these open habitats on the coast, until the development of arable farming brought into existence new habitats which they were able successfully to colonise. The weed species which appear to have been introductions into the flora by man have been discussed in earlier chapters; the native weed species seem most likely to have survived the Post-glacial forest period in coastal habitats.

In general, apart from the high montane grasslands and the steeper crags, coastal vegetation provides examples of the most natural and unmodified vegetation to be found in Britain today.

11 British vegetation history II. Wetlands

Wetlands, or "mires"

THE word "fen" is used botanically to denote a wet vegetation where the ground water-level is at the surface, and where the water is sufficiently rich in bases to produce a characteristic fen community of plants. Wet areas where the ground water is poor in dissolved bases, and so the soil is acid, develop quite a different plant community, and are called bog. Where the ground water is marginal in composition, a type of vegetation called "poor-fen" results. Bog vegetation found in valley bottoms or ill-drained hollows, where the water is poor in dissolved bases, is called "basin peat" or "topogenous peat". Bogs where the peat surface is above the ground water level, so that the plants depend on rainwater alone, are "ombrogenous", and are divided into "raised bogs", which are doomed in section, and built up on either old lake sediments or on impermeable clay substrata, and "blanket bogs", which are not domed in section but lie over flat land and moderate slopes as a mantle of peat. In addition to these types of ombrogenous peat, many upland areas of rather steep topography carry areas of ombrogenous peat which are localised to ground which is either completely flat, or is plastered with a spread of impermeable boulder clay; this peat is not domed, nor is it true blanket bog, and the author has proposed for it the term "topographic" peat.

All these types of wetland vegetation are sometimes referred to collectively by the term "mires". In northern England and southern Scotland, both raised bogs and blanket-bog fragments are called "mosses", reflecting the Scandinavian element in the place-names of this region. The common factor in all these vegetation types is that the wetness leads to anaerobic conditions in the substratum, and this means that vegetable remains are slow to decay because of inhibition of the micro-organisms causing decay. Hence a build-up of peat occurs. Many fens have in the course of time become converted into raised bogs by the build-up of the peat until it is above the ground-water level, but since ombrogenous peat forms only in an extremely oceanic climate, this succession is not found in the drier parts of the British Isles. The most extensive development of raised bogs is found in Ireland, and blanket peat is most widely found there, and on the flat Pennine summits above about 1200 feet, and over the whole of the north-west of Scotland, including the islands, where in many places it descends to sea level because of the highly oceanic climate.

The peat formed by the various fen and bog plant communities differs chemically, partly because of the different chemical composition of the peat-forming plants, and partly because of environmental differences. Fen and basin peats contain some mineral content, brought in by the ground-water, whereas ombrogenous peats are almost entirely made up of organic matter, and are normally much more acid.

The Fenland

This region, where fen vegetation is so general as to give a name to the whole area, lies inland from the Wash, including parts of the counties of Norfolk, Suffolk, Cambridgeshire, the Isle of Ely, Huntingdonshire and Lincolnshire. The ground level is so little above sea level that there is only a very small fall on the rivers, so they have little scouring action and their estuaries in the Wash tend to silt up; at the same time, tidal rise brings sea water far up the rivers, ponding back the drainage from the land. The deposits of this great basin consist of interdigitating wedges of fen peat and of marine silt or clay deposited by encroaching sea water. Since large-scale drainage works were begun in the seventeenth century, and sluices were built across the mouths of the main channels, the sea has on the whole been kept out, and most of the area is now under cultivation. Drainage of the fen peat did however result in shrinkage, both by loss of water and by oxidation of the peat as saturation was succeeded by aeration and the micro-flora of decomposition became active. This shrinkage of the peat has lowered the ground level by several feet below the level of the drainage dykes and rivers, so that these now flow between artificially raised banks, and water from the land has to be pumped up into the drainage channels. At first this was done by power from windmills, but these were later replaced by steam and then Diesel power. Only a few isolated patches of fen vegetation in its original state remain—one of the best-known of these is at Wicken Fen, north of Cambridge. The seaward fringe of silt fens, on the silt of the latest great marine transgression, of Romano-British date, is somewhat higher and better drained. Both silt fen and peat fen soils now, after suitable management, provide some of the most fertile and intensively cultivated arable land in Britain, and their productivity fully justifies the expense of continual pumping to drain the land.

The upland surrounding Fenland consists largely of calcareous rocks of the oolitic limestone and chalk series, and where glacial drift is present, this too is often calcareous. The water draining across the fenland area is therefore hard, rich in calcium and other dissolved bases. The Post-glacial history of the Fenland has been worked out in considerable detail, and has been shown to involve a complex stratigraphy conditioned by changing land and sea levels and shifting drainage channels. During the Boreal period the sea level relative to the land was lower, and the Fenland was in consequence better drained than at later stages; peat began to form only in channels and basins at this time, and the general swamping proceeded as the relative sea level rose.

In the surviving fragments of fen vegetation, as at Wicken, the dominant factor in determining the fen vegetation seems to be the type of management practised. Untouched fen seems to revert fairly rapidly to carr woodland wherever the winter water level is not above the stools of the bushes. This kind of fen has been managed in the past as "mowing marsh", and its vegetation is dominated by *Molinia*. If cutting is discontinued, it will revert to carr woodland. Ground where the water-table is higher, so that it is flooded in winter, has a natural vegetation of the reed (*Phragmites*) or the Great Sedge (*Cladium mariscus*), and both these plants formed an important part of the fen economy, being harvested annually for reed thatch. ("Norfolk thatch" uses *Phragmites* for the main cover, with a ridge-pattern carried out in *Cladium*; *Cladium* is most durable, but expensive.) If reed or sedge areas dry out because of drainage, or if the *Molinia* marsh is left unmown, the shrubs which colonise these habitats to form carr are the alder buckthorn (*Frangula alnus*), the grey sallow (*Salix atrocinerea*), common buckthorn (*Rhamnus catharticus*) and guelder rose (*Viburnum opulus*). Privet, hawthorn and blackthorn also occur. Alder is not apparently a natural constituent of the carr at Wicken, though planted alders flourish and regenerate; this absence is surprising, in view of the abundance of alder pollen in the fen peats. In somewhat similar fens in the Norfolk Broads area, alder is the dominant tree in forming carr.

The general stratigraphic succession in the southern Fenland is that of a Lower Peat, overlain by a marine clay, the Fen Clay or Buttery Clay, which is in turn overlain by an Upper Peat. In the peat fens, the Upper Peat is exposed at the surface, but to seaward it is overlain by the Upper Silt, the deposit of a marine transgression in Romano-British times, which wedges out to landward. The Lower Peat began to form in channels and in basins during Boreal times, but gradually extended as the surface of the land became wetter. Near the base of the Lower Peat at some sites is a layer containing Mesolithic flint artifacts, and nearer its top is a Neolithic layer, now dated by objects and charcoal found at the site at Peacock's Farm, Shippea Hill. At this site a sand ridge provided a settlement site, from which rubbish fell into the peat accumulating in the adjacent channel. Above the Lower Peat is the Fen Clay, now dated by radiocarbon at the Shippea Hill site to between about 3000 B.C. and 2300 B.C. and representing a marine transgression which brought sea water far into the Fenland, so that the Fen Clay extends almost to the Fenland margins. During the Bronze Age there was a marine recession, and the Upper Peat began to be deposited in fens developed on the wet surface of the Fen Clay. These fens, built up on the surface of this clay, became floristically poorer and more oligotrophic, and in places, above the ground water level, *Sphagnum*-dominated vegetation and raised bogs developed. In the latter part of the Bronze Age, the peat surface became drier and was colonised by trees, particularly pine. During Romano-British times, it is known from historical sources that the first attempts by man were made to drain the surface of the drier parts of the Fenland margin, and the rich soil was cultivated for corn crops. In later Romano-British times, however, a second marine incursion brought the salt water far inland, and led to swamping of the peat surfaces of the parts not covered by the sea. In places great shallow meres of fresh water were formed, and in general, growth of the Upper Peat began once more. The remains of the Sub-Boreal forest must have been buried by an earlier stimulus to the growth of peat—possibly the increased oceanicity of the climate beginning in the centuries around 500 B.C. Through later and medieval times the fens must have remained ill-drained and virtually trackless, separating the Benedictine monasteries on the hill-islands in the waste, at Crowland, Thorney, Ely, Peterborough and Chatteris, which unlike the Cistercians, did not attempt any progressive programme of land use. The medieval fenmen developed a specialised way of life in which fishing and fowling on the great meres of Whittlesea and Trundle must have played a part, and must have become habituated to the fenmens' ague—malaria. But in 1600 an Act was passed "for the recovering of many hundred thousand acres of marshes", and during the seventeenth century the reclamation began.

Esthwaite Fen

At the north end of Esthwaite Water in north Lancashire is a fen which illustrates the development of a normal hydrosere, which has here filled in the shallow inflow end of the lake with about 2 metres of peat on top of about 12 metres of lake mud. The vegetation succession here forms an illustration of comparatively recent changes (see the pollen diagram in Fig. 25) with little trace of man's influence in these pollen spectra. The various degrees of silting which have taken place on the fen can be correlated with differences in vegetation types, and within the one area are included various "mire" communities ranging from true fen to incipient bog. The water of this fen is somewhat acid (pH *c.* 5.5), draining off base-poor Silurian slates, but many of the true-fen species—using the alkaline fens of East Anglia as the criterion of "true fen"—are found, presumably because of the influence of the silt on the composition of the peat. The silting arises from periodic flooding of the inflow stream, with consequent deposition on parts of the peat of water-borne silt.

The areas of rapid silting, which have a ratio of organic to inorganic matter in the peat of not more than 1.3, carry a vegetation of reedswamp (*Typha latifolia* and *Phragmites*) or of mixed fen with *Typha, Phalaris arundinacea, Carex elata, Menyanthes trifoliata, Iris pseudacorus* and *Galium palustre,* with

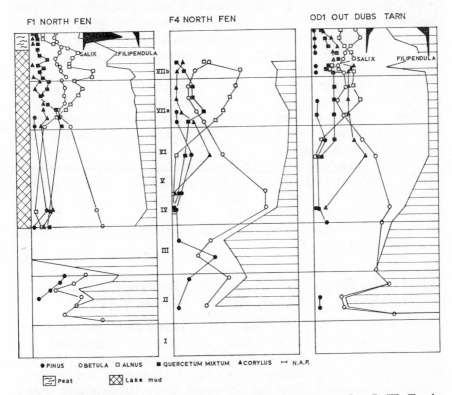

Figure 25. Pollen diagrams from Esthwaite Fen, N. Lancs, after J. W. Franks. Reproduced by permission of the *New Phytologist* from J. W. Franks and W. Pennington, **60,** 1961.

Phragmites, and bushes of *Salix atrocinerea* and *Salix purpurea.* Along the streamside itself is a community of *Phalaris,* with *Calamagrostis canescens* and *Filipendula ulmaria.* These are all typical fen species.

In areas of moderate silting, the ratio of organic to inorganic matter in the peat is between 1.5 and 2.2. The vegetation is reedswamp, of *Phragmites* and *Scirpus lacustris,* or a belt of sedges dominated by *Carex elata,* or open or closed carr of alder, birch, *Salix atrocinerea* and *Salix purpurea;* in the closed carr, *Salix atrocinerea* is dominant. There is a long list of associated species, many of which occur also in the East Anglian fens. *Eriophorum angustifolium* is an interesting plant in both lists; it is more often found on acid bogs. There is little or no trace of regeneration in the carr—no new young willow bushes are to be seen.

The areas of slow silting, where the ratio of organic to inorganic matter in the peat is 1·76, changed strikingly between 1914 and 1929; they carry a vegetation of *Scirpus lacustris* and *Phragmites* in the water, and Molinietum as the water level falls. This community is in striking contrast to the other vegetation types, because of the poverty of species—apart from *Molinia*; it contains only *Galium saxatile*, *Potentilla erecta*, *Succisa pratensis*, *Myrica gale*, the fern *Dryopteris dilatata*, and *Sphagnum acutifolium*. It forms a transition from fen to bog.

Pearsall, who described this vegetation, considered that in conditions of oceanic climate and with waters draining from mainly acidic rocks, the communities resembling those of fens are very transitory, and can only develop where there is abundant inorganic silting. Molinietum clearly forms a transition stage between fen and bog.

The pollen diagram from a profile on Esthwaite North Fen, in Fig. 25, shows how recently in the Post-glacial history of the site must this vegetation succession have been initiated. In many Post-glacial profiles, there is a stratigraphic succession through lake sediment, then fen peat, and then bog peat. Professor Pearsall believed that the transitory fen stage is there to be studied at present on Esthwaite Fen.

Raised bogs: Shapwick Heath, Tregaron Bog, the Lonsdale Mosses, the Silver Flowe, and Irish raised bogs of the Central Plain

In several previous chapters we have been concerned with the evidence on Post-glacial vegetation history supplied by profiles from raised bogs, particularly Tregaron Bog in Wales, those of the Somerset levels such as Shapwick Heath, and the Lonsdale mosses round Morecambe Bay, including Thrang Moss, Ellerside Moss and Helsington Moss. In the history of these great domes of peat, a fen stage of reedswamp or carr woodland was transitory and passed over into an acid bog vegetation, consisting largely of *Sphagnum* species. During the drier climate of the Sub-Boreal period the peat-forming plants included other species, notably *Calluna* and *Eriophorum*, and the margins of some of the bogs were colonised by pine and birch; in general, the peat grew more slowly and became more highly humified, and it is possible that some erosion took place. In all these bogs there are pronounced recurrence surfaces of the Weber type, which have been dated by radiocarbon to the centuries between 800 and 500 B.C. Above the recurrence surfaces the peat is fresh and unhumified, consisting entirely of *Sphagnum* species, including the highly oceanic *Sphagnum imbricatum*.

The present state of these bogs is far from uniform. Shapwick Heath,

Plate 22. *Gentiana verna* (Spring Gentian), the Burren, County Clare. M. C. F. Proctor.

Plate 23. *Artemisia norvegica* var. scotica, Scotland. J. E. Louseley. (Reproduced by permission of Collins from Plate XIIb, *Mountain Flowers*, by John Raven and Max Walters.)

Plate 24. *Koenigia islandica*, Scotland. J. E. Raven. (Reproduced by permission of Collins from Plate XII, *Mountain Flowers*, by John Raven and Max Walters.)

Plate 25. *Agropyron donianum*, Inchnadamph, Scotland. J. E. Raven. (Reproduced by permission of Collins from Plate XVIIb, *Mountain Flowers*, by John Raven and Max Walters.)

Plate 26. *Minuartia stricta* (Bog sandwort). Teesdale. M. C. F. Proctor. (Reproduced by permission of Collins from Plate VIIb, *Mountain Flowers*, by John Raven and Max Walters.)

Plate 27. *Carex capillaris*, Clova mountains, Scotland. M. C. F. Proctor. (Reproduced by permission of Collins from Plate VIIb, *Mountain Flowers*, by John Raven and Max Walters.)

Plate 28. *Rumex longifolius*, A dock. J. E. Lousley.

Plate 29. *Smyrnium olusatrum*, a naturalised, originally introduced, plant. Cornwall.

Plate 30. *Matricaria matricarioides*, a recent introduction. (Reproduced by permission of Collins from Plate VIII, *Weeds and Aliens*, by Sir Edward Salisbury.)

described by Godwin as a "derelict" raised bog, apparently ceased to grow in late Roman times. Parts of Tregaron, and the Lonsdale mosses, have been extensively cut for peat and drained around the margins, so that much of their surface is in a condition which must be far from natural. This applies to a great many of the British raised bogs, and reflects the importance of peat as a fuel before the days of cheap coal. Drained or derelict raised bogs are usually covered with a vegetation dominated by *Calluna*, and may have birch and pine trees. Where the surface is less modified, *Eriophorum vaginatum* accompanies *Calluna*, and where the water table is still near the surface, *Sphagnum* species are still found, accompanied by such plants as *Erica tetralix* (Cross-leaved Heath), Deer sedge (*Trichophorum cespitosum*), the bog rosemary (*Andromeda polifolia*) and the cranberry (*Vaccinium oxycoccus*).

The raised bogs of which the surface is still growing upwards (or "living"), are on the whole in the more remote or more oceanic parts of Britain. The West bog at Tregaron is in this state, and so are many of the great bogs or "flowes" of Galloway, but the greatest concentration of living raised bogs is in the Central Irish plain (Plate 12). On a living bog surface there are many pools, in which grow aquatic species of *Sphagnum*, including *S. cuspidatum* and between them are raised hummocks formed by different species of *Sphagnum* (notably *S. rubellum*). The hummocks grow rapidly upwards and are colonised by various flowering plants and lichens—*Calluna*, *Eriophorum vaginatum* and *E. angustifolium*, *Trichophorum cespitosum*, *Erica tetralix*, *Rhynchospora alba*, *Narthecium ossifragum* (Bog Asphodel) and *Cladonia*. A bog of which the surface is sufficiently unmodified to show a pool and hummock structure usually still shows its steep boundary slope down to the marginal drainage channel, the "lagg", where fen vegetation may have developed. It is obvious that in such a bog, the water in the pools, being above ground water level, is held only by the peat, which may be in a state of tension. If the bog is on sloping ground, the tension will be greater. Those bogs which have many large pools on their surface often show a distinct alignment of the pools, which are elongated along a line at right angles to the direction of slope of the peat surface. The nature and origin of the pools on these large growing bogs is still not fully understood by ecologists. The small pools, with hummocks between them, form what is called the pool and hummock complex, and the theory which seems to fit the state of affairs on many bogs, originally propounded by Osvald in Sweden, is that the upward growth of the hummocks reaches a limit as the top becomes drier, and it then passes into a vegetation of old *Calluna* and the lichen *Cladonia*, which becomes subject to wind erosion, so that the top of the old hummock is somewhat lowered. Meanwhile the intervening small pools, full of aquatic *Sphagna*, have been growing upwards rapidly, and continue their growth until they overtop the degenerating old hummock, the site of which then becomes a new pool. As the former pools grow upwards, the species of *Sphagnum* will change, from the aquatic species to the hummock-formers. This theory of pool and hummock regeneration of the bog surface was considered by Godwin and Conway to fit the state of affairs to be observed on the surface of the West bog at Tregaron.

Other workers, Ratcliffe and Walker on the Silver Flowe, and Walker and Walker in the Irish bogs, have however found pools which are larger than those of the observed pool and hummock complex, and in the Irish bogs the Walkers found traces of these large pools preserved in profile in peat cuttings. The mud of these large pools, one or more metres in diameter, containing remains of *Sphagnum cuspidatum*, can be seen to transgress in the profile across remains of both hummock and small pool peat, showing that the large pools were not part of the pool and hummock regeneration complex. It would seem from all this research that the development of a large raised bog is dependent upon the integration of many factors; while it is possible to find profiles of Irish bogs in which the recent peat can be interpreted on the hypothesis of alternation of pool and hummock structure, as seen in Tansley, Table XXI, in other Irish bogs, as the Walkers have been able to show, there is considerable evidence for long periods of rather flattish bog surfaces, carrying uniform peat-forming vegetation of either pure *Sphagnum* communities or mixtures of *Sphagnum* and *Calluna*. The large pools which are present on the surface, and show up in the profiles as layers of mud with *S. cuspidatum*, in these latter bogs, seem to have been formed as a response to a general change in the hydrography of the bog as a whole, and the same explanation is considered to account for the large pools on the Silver Flowe. In Walker's view the large pools are quite distinct from the smaller pools of the pool and hummock complex. His opinion is that the surfaces of bogs like these are very susceptible to climatic change, but would under constant climatic conditions probably develop fairly uniform plant communities, with a reduction in the number of pools.

Blanket bogs: the Pennines, Scotland, Ireland, and Southern Pennines

The very extensive almost level summits of the Pennines carry great expanses of blanket bog, and perhaps the most striking feature of this peat is the erosion to which it is now subject. The thick mantle of peat is now dissected by an intricate series of drainage channels, in the sides of which the peat profile is exposed, and the floors of which are cut down to the underlying mineral soil. In some places, erosion has proceeded so far that the peat cover has been stripped from quite extensive areas. The exposed sides and remaining islands of peat in a dissected system are called peat haggs. One of the questions most frequently asked of an historical ecologist is when and why did this erosion begin. Only a partial answer can as yet be given.

Conway (1954) in a classic paper based on field work in the Sheffield area, before radiocarbon dating had been developed, demonstrated that the growth of the blanket peat began there at the beginning of the Atlantic period—that is, about 7500 B.P., at altitudes above 1200 feet where drainage was poor, and that peat growth thereafter extended, the rate of upward growth of the peat having been much greater in the last two millennia than previously. Her conclusion was that in this last period of very rapid growth of *Sphagnum* peat, "the peat blanket tended to develop its own drainage system, and became readily subject to erosion". She divided the summit peats into three main layers: "(i) The Basal Peat, highly humified, lacking *Sphagnum*, and sometimes containing wood. This layer is rarely over 50 cm thick, and usually about 30 cm." [This seems to correspond broadly with the layer containing wood at the base of the Lake District blanket peat, shown in Fig. 23.] (ii) Uniform peat with *Sphagnum* abundant but not conspicuous in the field. The layer appears uniform in the field except for tufts of *Eriophorum vaginatum* remains, which are especially abundant towards the top of the layer. This and the Basal Peat together may conveniently be called the Lower Peat in contrast to: (iii) The Upper Peat which is much less compact, and usually shows banding, or alternation between fresh *Sphagnum* peat layers and more humified layers" (Conway, 1954).

Within the thickness of the Upper Peat, Conway found typical "recurrence surfaces", and showed convincing evidence for equating the most pronounced of these with the Grenz horizon, the beginning of the Sub-Atlantic period. "Since 500 B.C. climatic conditions on the summit of the southern Pennines have been wet enough to produce fresh *Sphagnum* peat, and erosion has therefore been likely to set in at any time since that date." (Conway, *op cit.*)

Conway further deals with the phenomenon of "healing", which is a recolonisation by *Sphagna* of hollows and ditches in the drainage system, and can be seen in bogs of the Northern Pennines and Scotland, but not in the Southern Pennines. Pearsall believed that burning of the surface vegetation, as practised on grouse moors, has a selectively destructive effect on *Sphagna*, and the absence of healing *Sphagna* from the Southern Pennines may be related to their position between densely populated areas.

The absence of *Sphagnum* healing in the erosion gullies of the Southern Pennines is only part of a general difference between their vegetation and that of more northerly or westerly blanket bogs. Though the peat, except for the surface few centimetres, is made up of remains of *Sphagnum*, the bogs are now dominated by *Eriophorum vaginatum*, and *Sphagnum* is rare. This problem is reviewed by Pearsall in "Mountains and Moorlands", and he attributes the change in vegetation to draining and burning, which the other regions of blanket bog have not suffered so intensely. Since *Eriophorum* is characteristic of bog surfaces which are drier than those made up of *Sphagnum*, it is possible, as Conway points out, that in the years since 1800 A.D. the climate of the area has been drier than previously, but Pearsall regarded the draining and burning as likeliest to account for the change in vegetation. Tallis has recently investigated the Pennine peat near Manchester, both by pollen analysis and by detailed identification of the *Sphagnum* remains. In the Upper Peat he finds the same type of consistent "recurrence surface" as Conway, and by close analysis of *Sphagnum* species, has been able to show that these horizons are characterised by a succession from species characteristic of a drying bog surface, to species which inhabit the pools on a wet bog surface. It is above the level of the topmost of these recurrence surfaces that *Eriophorum vaginatum* appears in quantity, and since its appearance is accompanied by a great increase in the pollen of *Plantago* and total non-tree pollen, it is assumed that this marks the beginning of permanent human settlement and land exploitation. It has not yet been dated by radiocarbon, but Tallis suggests that it was some time after the fourteenth century by the time *Eriophorum vaginatum* had become dominant in the peat-forming vegetation and *Sphagnum* had begun to decline. The theory that burning of the vegetation was the reason for the decline in *Sphagnum* receives support from the fact that Tallis found charcoal in the peat from this time on. In the topmost 2–3 cm of peat, soot is present in quantity, undoubtedly from atmospheric pollution, and this layer is interpreted as the deposit of the time since about 1800 A.D. In the sooty layer there are no traces of *Sphagnum* at all. It seems reasonable to suppose, therefore, that the present cotton-sedge moors of the South Pennine blanket bogs constitute a vegetation type entirely due to the influence of man, derived by human activity from the *Sphagnum* vegetation which had been there for several thousand years. Now there is only the hardy cotton-sedge, "rooted in soot and watered by dilute sulphuric acid", as another ecologist remarked.

Northern Pennines

The blanket bog of Bowland Forest, Stainmoor, and the far northern Pennines has been described both in "Mountains and Moorlands", and in the Nature Conservancy's monograph on the Geology of Moor House. In their present vegetation cover *Calluna* tends to be dominant, but there is still much *Sphagnum*, and a richer flora of associated plants than on the cotton-sedge moors of the South Pennines. The associated plants include the bog-rosemary (*Andromeda polifolia*), (a beautiful plant whose disappearance from the South Pennines, since 1835 when it was described as "abundant", has been recorded), *Erica tetralix, Narthecium ossifragum,* sundews, and other plants which are also found on growing raised bogs. Both species of cotton-sedge are also present. The peat of these bogs is of *Sphagnum–Eriophorum–Calluna*, with a layer of buried wood, birch with willow and juniper, at the base. On the Moor House Nature Reserve, there seems to have been a light forest of these trees up to a height of about 2500 feet during the Boreal period. At that time peat was forming only in ill-drained hollows, but as in the Southern Pennines, with the change to a wetter climate at the opening of the Atlantic period, blanket peat began to form, and spread until even the highest fells were peat-covered. On the flat tops of Cross and Knock Fells, this peat lies directly over stone polygons. An extremely interesting feature is the inclusion in this peat of microliths of Mesolithic type. Some of them lie on the mineral soil at the base of the peat, and may be of Boreal age, and some are included in the Atlantic peat. With them have been found the horn-sheaths of wild cattle, and it is supposed that wandering bands of Mesolithic hunters must have frequented the high moors before the enveloping growth of blanket peat began. Those horn-sheaths found at these levels in the peat have been referred tentatively to the Urus (*Bos taurus primigenius*), which was presumably the quarry of these hunters.

The northern Pennine blanket bogs have been eroded in the same way as those in the south just discussed. "All the continuous peat cover over 2500 feet has been removed by erosion, and widespread peat erosion is now present below this height. Another factor which strongly favours the correlation of the beginning of peat erosion with the Sub-Atlantic climatic deterioration concerns the increase in rainfall. The influence of waterlogging in producing instability and erosion of deep blanket bog has been stressed . . . The climatic change from dry to wet would cause saturation of the blanket bog on the exposed high fells, and on sloping ground this would inevitably lead to instability and the start of peat erosion" (Johnson and Dunham, 1963).

Scotland

The plant associations of the Scottish blanket bogs have been described by McVean and Ratcliffe in "Plant Communities of the Scottish Highlands", the first Nature Conservancy monograph. Blanket bog is now the climax vegetation over vast areas of north-west Scotland and the islands, since the Sub-Atlantic climate is there so highly oceanic with low summer temperatures, heavy rainfall and high humidity, that blanket peat forms even at sea level on moderate slopes, so that only the exceptionally well-drained land is free of peat. Outstanding examples of blanket bog are the Moor of Rannoch, Perthshire, and Strathy Bog in north Sutherland, but north-west of the Great Glen it is impossible to travel far without being aware of vast stretches which, if not bare rock, are blanket bog. Much of the deer forest country is covered by a thin skin of blanket peat, which becomes thick peat in any hollow. The vegetation of the Scottish blanket bogs is characteristically of *Calluna*, both cotton sedges, deer sedge (*Trichophorum cespitosum*), *Erica tetralix*, Purple Moor Grass (*Molinia caerulea*), Sweet Gale (*Myrica gale*), Bog Asphodel (*Narthecium ossifragum*) and sundews, but dominated by species of *Sphagnum*. On Rannoch Moor there is *Scheuchzeria palustris*, a plant which was common in Britain at the time of the flooding of bog surfaces at the opening of the

Sub-Atlantic period, but has disappeared from all its other localities during the last hundred years.

Many of the higher Scottish bogs are dominated almost completely by *Calluna* and *Trichophorum cespitosum*. In the east their vegetation is somewhat different from that of the western bogs, having more ericoid plants—*Empetrum*, *Vaccinium* species, including *V. microcarpum* (the small cranberry), and *Arctostaphylos uva-ursi* (the Bearberry).

Traces of forest buried in the Scottish blanket peat are abundant, and clearly both pine and birch forests have perished in this way. Early descriptions, before the development of the technique of pollen analysis, suggested that there may be two distinct horizons at which forests were overcome by peat, and it seemed reasonable to suppose that the two periods of rapid growth of peat were respectively the Atlantic and the Sub-Atlantic. As explained in earlier chapters, however, analysis of many peat profiles containing buried wood has not confirmed this theory. Regressional changes from forest to bog have progressed at different rates depending primarily on local conditions and soil drainage, rather than on synchronous climatic change. At some sites there is no trace of human influence, while at others anthropogenic effects are clear.

Ireland

The extreme west of Ireland resembles north-west Scotland in its highly oceanic climate, and has a similar climatic climax vegetation of blanket bog on all flat and gently sloping ground. Peat growth seems to have gone on in Ireland continuously since about 2000 B.C., and though the ombrogenous peat contains records of flooding of the bog surface (as discussed in the previous section, on raised bogs) which is in one sense a minor recurrence surface, there are no major recurrence surfaces which can be correlated from one bog to another (Walker & Walker 1961). This of course applies also to the raised bogs. It would seem that within the limits of Ireland's particularly oceanic climate, there has at no time been a period when peat growth was so slow as to form a major retardation layer. On the other hand, the onset of even wetter conditions in the Sub-Atlantic did extend the area of blanket peat, and forests were overcome and buried in this peat, as shown in Plate 10. In many places in Ireland the subsequent growth of peat has also entombed and preserved early prehistoric sites, including cultivated fields.

The *Sphagna* which dominate the Irish blanket bogs are mainly *S. papillosum* and *S. rubellum*. The flowering plants are varying proportions of the following, with some bogs dominated by *Rhynchospora alba* (White beak sedge) and some by *Molinia*. Other plants are *Eriophorum vaginatum*, *Trichophorum cespitosum* and *Schoenus nigricans*, with occasional occurrence of most of the other bog plants which have been mentioned.

12 Some plants with interesting distributions

Betula nana (Dwarf birch), Fig. 26 and Plate 17

THE very striking "relict" distribution of this plant has already been mentioned several times. It has been recorded at sites in many parts of Britain in Late-glacial and early Post-glacial deposits, but is now found only on Scottish mountains and at the single locality in Upper Teesdale where it was discovered only very recently. In north-west Europe it has similar relict stations in the French Jura, and on Lüneberg Heath, where remains of it can be found in the ombrogenous peat on which the plant is growing, all the way down the profile to the Late-glacial layers. This site is about 500 km from the nearest other site, in the Harz mountains.

Betula nana comes within the Arctic-alpine group of plants, being found at both high latitudes in the northern hemisphere, and at high altitudes in the Alps. It can form hybrids with the tree birches, *Betula pubescens* and *B. tortuosa*; such hybrids are reported from Iceland by Löve and Löve, are frequent in the Äbisko district of northern Sweden, but are said to be rare in Norway (Faegri). In Britain, hybrids between *B. nana* and *B. pubescens* are known only from two localities in Scotland, on Ben Loyal and in Glen Clova.

It seems proved beyond doubt that *Betula nana* was widespread over the lowlands of north-west Europe under Late-glacial conditions, but has been extinguished from all localities except on mountains (and, rarely, on peat substrata at lower altitudes) by the spread of forest trees—probably there is also some limiting temperature effect, but this is a plant tolerant of acid soils, so that the contraction of its range since the Late-glacial period bears no relation to the diminishing base-status of the soils.

Dryas octopetala (Mountain Avens), Fig. 27 and Plate 18

The present distribution of this plant in Britain has much in common with that of *Betula nana*, but it is less restricted to high mountain habitats, and is

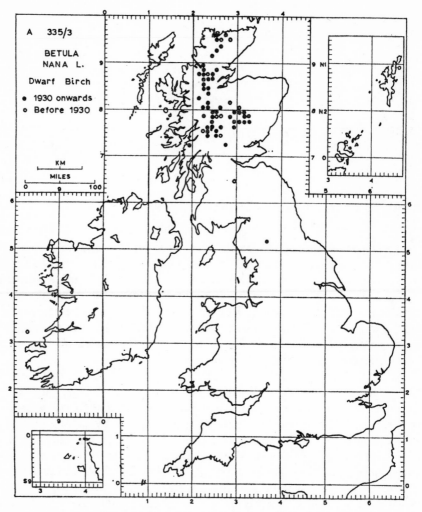

Figure 26. Distribution map—present distribution of *Betula nana*. Reproduced from "Atlas of the British Flora" by permission of the Botanical Society of the British Isles and of Thomas Nelson and Sons Ltd, Publishers, with the addition of the recent record from Upper Teesdale.

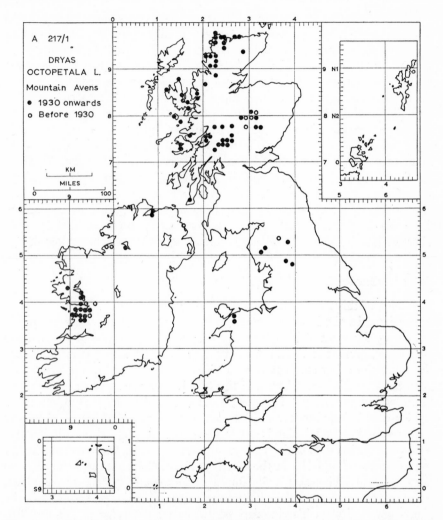

Figure 27. Distribution map—present distribution of *Dryas octopetala*. Reproduced from "Atlas of the British Flora" by permission of the Botanical Society of the British Isles and of Thomas Nelson and Sons Ltd, Publishers.

found only on base-rich soils. It belongs to the Arctic-Montane rather than the Arctic-Alpine group. During the Late-glacial period it was, like *Betula nana*, widespread in the lowlands of Britain and the rest of north-west Europe. Dahl supposes it to be confined at present to sites where the July isotherm does not exceed 27°C., and if this is indeed always true for this plant, its Late-glacial distribution gives a useful indication of summer temperatures in Lowland Britain at this time. It is one of the plants recorded from Full-glacial deposits, as is *Betula nana*, and it is possible that both of these species could have survived in Britain all through the Weichsel Glaciation.

Dryas octopetala is now found on mountain ledges, as on the Helvellyn range at 2300 feet, and at sites in the Scottish Highlands, and a few places in the mountains of Wales and Ireland—in Snowdonia and on Ben Bulben— but it is also found at lower altitudes on base-rich soils, as in Teesdale and at calcareous sites near sea level—on the Burren, on the north coast of Suther-land at Bettyhill, and on the Durness Limestone of West Sutherland. At all these sites its apparent requirements of freedom from competition by trees, a base-rich soil, and low summer temperatures, are found in combination.

Salix herbacea (Least Willow), Fig. 28 and Plate 16

The third of this trio of characteristically Late-glacial plants which are now so restricted in distribution, *Salix herbacea*, is probably the easiest to find of the three, for most British botanists. It is widely dispersed on Scottish mountains, present at several places in the Lake District mountains, and has sites in Wales as far south as Brecon Beacons. In Ireland it has many sites, including Ben Bulben. Characteristically it is now more a plant of mountain summits than the two previous species. It also tends to have a more westerly distribution, being absent from Teesdale, and not recorded from Late-glacial deposits outside the Highland zone of Great Britain. In Ireland it had a very wide distribution during the Late-glacial period, being very common in the clays of Zones I and III, in the way that *Dryas* characterises these clays on the Continent. Though usually found in comparatively base-rich habitats, *Salix herbacea* can grow on soils poor in calcium, for it was recorded in the plant community on Torridonian sandstone on the ridge in Wester Ross where *Artemisia norvegica* was first discovered.

Salix herbacea is today widely found in the Arctic regions of the northern hemisphere, as well as in the Central European mountains, and is therefore a member of the Arctic-Alpine group of plants.

Koenigia islandica, Fig. 29 and Plate 24

This plant, a member of the Polygonaceae (the dock family), has been so recently recognised as a member of the British flora that it has no English

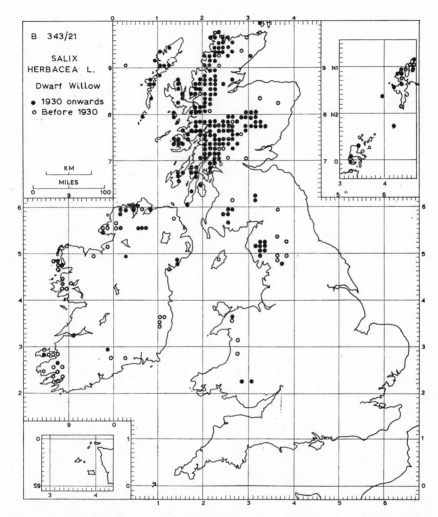

Figure 28. Distribution map—present distribution of *Salix herbacea*. Reproduced from "Atlas of the British Flora" by permission of the Botanical Society of the British Isles and of Thomas Nelson and Sons Ltd, Publishers.

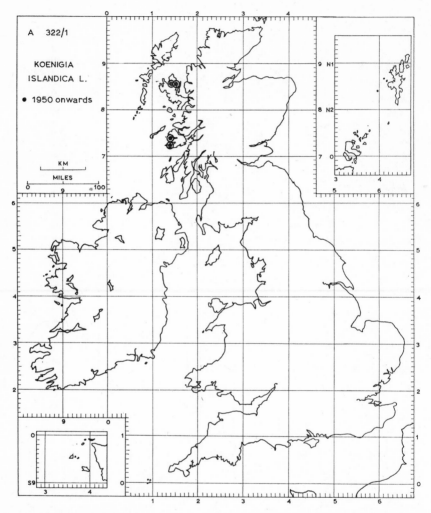

Figure 29. Distribution map—present distribution of *Koenigia islandica*. Reproduced from "Atlas of the British Flora" by permission of the Botanical Society of the British Isles and of Thomas Nelson and Sons Ltd, Publishers.

name. For a vivid account of its discovery, J. E. Raven's chapter on the "Volcanic hills of western Scotland" in the New Naturalist volume on Mountain Flowers should be consulted. As yet, *Koenigia* has only been found on the Storr range in northern Skye, and on Mull.

In 1956 Raven wrote "It is probably a glacial relict species, as the recent discovery of its pollen in the Late-glacial peat beds of Southern Scotland has conveniently confirmed". Pollen of *Koenigia* has now been found at other Late-glacial sites—by J. W. Franks, R. Andrew and D. Walker in the Lake District, by R. Andrew at Loch Droma, by H. J. B. Birks in Skye, and at several other sites.

"*Koenigia islandica* is a dwarf annual plant of circum-polar distribution, extending north almost to 80° in Spitzbergen . . . It also grows in the Southern hemisphere" (Godwin, 1956). It is a plant of very open habitats, common on frost-disturbed soils in the Arctic.

Papaver alpinum

Papaver alpinum, recorded from the Full-glacial Barnwell Station beds, had not been found since then in later deposits until fairly recently, when A. P. Conolly found in the Late-glacial deposits at Whitrig in Berwickshire a seed which can only be one of the arctic or alpine poppies, and which resembles that of *Papaver alpinum*. This is as yet the only known example of a plant which was present in the British flora during the Late-glacial period and then died out.

Naias marina, Fig. 30

The fruits of this plant have been recorded frequently in interglacial deposits, and for Full-glacial deposits in south-east England. It has not however been found in the Late-glacial flora. In view of the implications of the Post-glacial distribution of this plant, which is now found only at one or two localities in the Norfolk Broads, the Full-glacial records, as Godwin says, "require reconsideration". Possibly the fruits were secondary, derived from aquatic sediments of the previous interglacial.

The records of this plant in Post-glacial deposits come from several sites in Ireland, where it is now extinct, and from western England and Wales, as well as from the Norfolk region where it still grows. In Scandinavia also this plant had a much wider Post-glacial distribution, extending much further north, than the present. It seems to furnish an example of restriction in the range of the plant in the later Post-glacial period by lower temperatures. In this it resembles the distribution of the Great Sedge (*Cladium mariscus*) in Scandinavia.

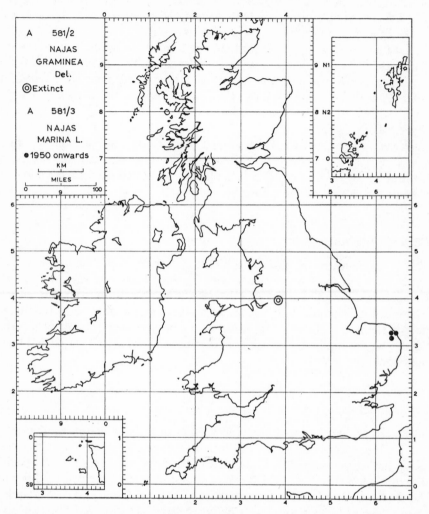

Figure 30. Distribution map—present distribution of *Naias marina*. Reproduced from "Atlas of the British Flora" by permission of the Botanical Society of the British Isles and of Thomas Nelson and Sons Ltd, Publishers.

Naias flexilis, Fig. 31

Fig. 31 shows the distribution, present and fossil, of *Naias flexilis* in Europe and North America. This plant is considered by Godwin and by Deevey to be one of circumpolar distribution, which was dispersed more widely and was more abundant in the early Post-glacial warm period than it is today. The fossil distribution in northern Scandinavia shows this very clearly. In Britain, this plant was abundant during the Boreal period, from which it is recorded, often in great quantity, at many places in Ireland, and in East Anglia, where it no longer grows. On the other hand, its occurrence today in several localities in northern Scotland suggests that its apparent absence now from most of England and from south-east Ireland is not purely a temperature effect (reflecting decrease in warmth since the early Post-glacial warm period) but that other factors are involved.

Scheuchzeria palustris, Fig. 32

This plant shows an example of restricted range at present, in the extreme form—that is, it is now found at only one place in the British Isles, compared with a much wider distribution in the early Sub-Atlantic. Before that there is no record for it in the Post-glacial period. At the time of the major climatic shift, between 800 and 500 B.C., *Scheuchzeria* must have been abundant in the vegetation of the pools on the wet bog surfaces, and its remains can be found forming a distinct layer in the peat at the base of the fresh Sub-Atlantic peat. In Somerset, there is a later layer in the peat representing a flooding horizon, and again *Scheuchzeria* is abundant in it. During the last few centuries, draining and cutting of the great raised bogs must have reduced very seriously the habitats available to *Scheuchzeria*; until quite recently it was growing on some of the Shropshire raised bogs, and on some in Yorkshire, but now its only locality is on the Moor of Rannoch. This is therefore an example of a plant brought to the verge of extinction by human activity.

The Lusitanian-Mediterranean element in south-west Ireland

This consists of a number of plant species which in Britain are found only in the extreme south-west of Ireland, and outside Britain inhabit the western Mediterranean region. Characteristic species are *Arbutus unedo*, the Strawberry Tree, *Saxifraga hirsuta*, *Erica hibernica* (*mediterranea*), *Erica vagans* *Erica mackiana*, *Daboecia cantabrica*, *Pinguicula grandiflora* and *Pinguicula lusitanica*. This "Lusitanian" flora seems to have extended north along the Atlantic seaboard, and to have found its furthest outpost in the extreme south-west of Ireland. *Erica vagans* is found also in Cornwall.

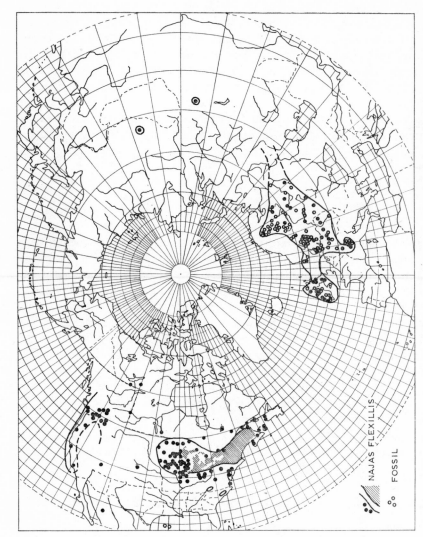

Figure 31. Distribution map—present distribution of *Naias flexilis*. Reproduced from "Amphi-Atlantic Plants" by E. Hulten, by permission of the Swedish Academy of Science.

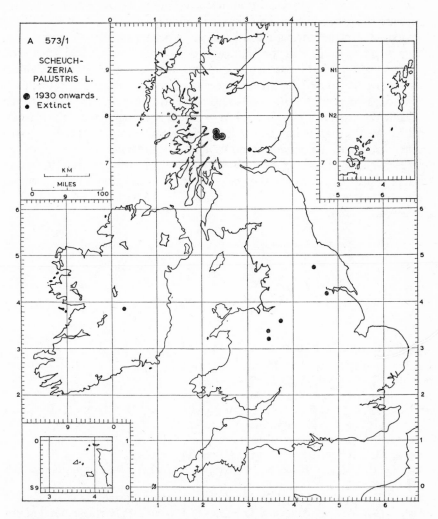

Figure 32. Distribution map—present distribution of *Scheuchzeria palustris*. Reproduced from "Atlas of the British Flora" by permission of the Botanical Society of the British Isles and of Thomas Nelson and Sons Ltd, Publishers.

The question of the history of this group of plants has of course attracted great interest, and as yet remains an unsolved problem. *Arbutus* and certain others are so susceptible to frost that it is unbelievable that they could have survived in Ireland through the Weichsel glaciation. The most probable theory seems to be that in the very early post-glacial period, while sea level may have been 300 feet lower than it is today (since large parts of the Scandinavian, and particularly the North American, ice-caps remained unmelted), land bridges between not only the Continent and Great Britain, but between England, Wales and Ireland, would be exposed, and migration of these frost-sensitive species might then have taken place along coastal fringes long since submerged, where the climate could well have been an oceanic variant of the early Post-glacial climate in general, and so have permitted the migration and survival of these plants. As the sea level rose, these coastal fringes would become submerged, leaving this flora isolated in the highly oceanic corner of south-west Ireland.

Further Reading

Added to Second Edition

Bell, Frances G. (1969). *New Phytol.*, **68**, 913–922.

Birks, Hilary H. (1970). *J. Ecol.*, **58**, 827–846.

Birks, Hilary H. (1972). *New Phytol.*, **71**, 731–754.

Birks, H. J. B. (1973). *Past and present vegetation of the Isle of Skye.* C.U.P.

Boulter, M. C. (1971). *Bulletin Brit. Mus. (Nat. Hist.) Geology*, 19, No. 7.

Clark, J. G. D. (1971). *Excavations at Star Carr.* C.U.P.

Clark, R. M. and Renfrew, C. (1973). *Nature*, **243**, 266–270.

Coope, G. R. (1970a). *Revue de Geographie Physique et de Géologie Dynamique* **XII**, 149–155.

Coope, G. R. (1970b). *Annual Review of Entomology*, **15**, 97–120.

Coope, G. R., Morgan, Anne and Osborne, P. J. (1971). *Palaeogeography Palaeoclimatology, Palaeoecology*, **10**, 87–101.

Hibbert, F. A., Switsur, V. R. and West, R. G. (1971). *Proc. Roy. Soc. Lond.*, **B177**, 161–171.

Moore, P. D. (1973). *Nature*, **241**, 350–353.

Pennington, W., Haworth, E. Y., Bonny, A. P. and Lishman, J. P. (1972). *Phil. Trans. Roy. Soc. Lond.*, **B264**, 191–294.

Pennington, W. and Bonny, A. P. (1970). *Nature*, **226**, 871–3.

Penny, L. F., Coope, G. R. and Catt, J. A. (1969). *Nature*, **224**, 65–7.

Sparks, B. W. and West, R. G. (1972). *The Ice Age in Britain*, Methuen.

Turner, C. (1970). *Phil. Trans. Roy. Soc. Lond.*, **B257**, 373–440.

Walker, D. and West, R. G. (Edit.) (1970). *Studies in the Vegetational History of the British Isles*. C.U.P. (reference is made to the contributions of A. G. Smith, J. Turner and W. Pennington).

West, R. G. (1968). *Pleistocene Geology and Biology*, Longmans.

West, R. G. (1970). *New Phytol.*, **69**, 1179–1183.

West, R. G. (1971). *Studying the Past by Pollen Analysis*, Oxford Biology Readers, O.U.P.

General

Godwin, H. (1956). *The History of the British Flora*. Cambridge University Press, 384 pp.

Linnean Society, London (1961). "Symposium on Quaternary Ecology". *Proc. Linn. Soc. Lond.*, **172**, pp. 25–89.

Perring, F. H. and Walters, S. M. (Ed.) (1962). *Atlas of the British Flora*. B.S.B.I. and Nelson, 432 pp.

Tansley, A. G. (1939). *The British Islands and their Vegetation*. Cambridge University Press, 930 pp.

Tansley, A. G. (1968). *Britain's Green Mantle* Second Edition, revised by M. C. F. Proctor. George Allen and Unwin Ltd., 297 pp.

The Pleistocene period

Andersen, S. Th. (1964). "Interglacial Plant Successions in the light of environmental changes". *Rep. VIth Int. Congress on the Quaternary, Warsaw*. Vol. 2, pp. 359–367.

Coope, G. R. (1962). "A Pleistocene Coleopterous Fauna". *Q.J.G.S.*, **118**, pp. 102–123.

Coope, G. R. (1965). "Fossil Insect Faunas from late Quaternary deposits in Britain". *Advancement of Science*, March 1965.

Faegri, K. and Iversen, J. (1964). *A Textbook of Pollen Analysis*. Blackwell, 237 pp.

Flint, R. F. (1957). *Glacial and Pleistocene Geology*. John Wiley & Sons Inc., 553 pp.

Davis, Margaret B. (1963). "On the theory of pollen analysis". *Amer. Jour. Sci.*, **261**, pp. 897–912.

Pearson, Ronald (1964). *Animals and Plants of the Cenozoic era*. Butterworths, 236 pp.

West, R. G. (1961). "Interglacial and Interstadial vegetation in England". *Proc. Linn. Soc. Lond.*, **172**, pp. 81–89.

West, R. G. (1963). "Problems of the British Quaternary". *Proc. Geol. Ass.*, **74**, pp. 147–186.

West, R. G. and Wilson, D. Gay (1966). "Cromer Forest Bed Series". *Nature*, **209**, pp. 497–498.

Zeuner, F. E. (1958). *Dating the Past*. Methuen, 516 pp.

Full- and Late-Weichselian vegetation

Conolly, A. P., Godwin, H. and Megaw, E. M. (1950). "Late-glacial deposits in Cornwall". *Phil. Trans. Roy. Soc.*, **B234**, pp. 397–469.

Bartley, D. D. (1962). "The stratigraphy and pollen analysis of lake deposits near Tadcaster, Yorkshire". *New Phytologist*, **61**, pp. 277–287.

Godwin, H. (1964). "Late-Weichselian conditions in south-eastern Britain: organic deposits at Colney Heath, Herts". *Proc. Roy. Soc.*, **B160**, pp. 258–275.

Jessen, K. (1949). "Studies in late-Quaternary deposits and the flora-history of Ireland". *Proc. Roy. Irish Acad.*, **B52**, pp. 6–85.

Jessen, K. and Farrington, A. (1938). "The bogs at Ballybetagh, near Dublin". *Proc. Roy. Irish Acad.*, **B44**, pp. 10–205.

Kirk, W. and Godwin, H. (1963). "A late-glacial site at Loch Droma, Ross and Cromarty". *Trans. Roy. Soc. Edin.*, **65**, pp. 225–249.

Lambert, C. A., Pearson, R. G. and Sparks, B. W. (1963). "A flora and fauna from late-Pleistocene deposits at Sidgwick Avenue, Cambridge". *Proc. Linn. Soc. Lond.*, **174**, **1**, 13.

Manley, G. (1959). "The late-glacial climate of north-west England". *Liv. and Manch. Geol. Journ.*, **2**, pp. 188–215.

Mitchell, G. F. (1960). "The Pleistocene history of the Irish Sea". *Pres. Addr. Section C. Brit. Ass. Adv. Science, Cardiff.*

Seddon, B. (1962). "Late-glacial deposits at Llyn Dwythwch and Nant Ffrancon, Caernarvonshire". *Phil. Trans. Roy. Soc.*, **B244**, pp. 459–481.

Van der Hammen, Th. (1957). "The Stratigraphy of the Late-glacial". *Geologie en Mijnbouw* (*NW Ser.*), *Symposium* 1957.

Post-glacial Vegetation

Conway, V. M. (1954). "Stratigraphy and Pollen Analysis of Southern Pennine blanket peats". *J. Ecol.*, **42**, pp. 1–117.

Iversen, J. (1960). "Problems of the Early Post-glacial Forest Development in Denmark". *Geological Survey of Denmark.* IV Series **4**, No. 3, 32 pp.

Godwin, H., Walker, D. and Willis, E. H. "Radiocarbon dating and post-glacial vegetational history: Scaleby Moss". *Proc. Roy. Soc.*, **B147**, pp. 352–365.

Pearsall, W. H. (Ed.) (1965). "A discussion on the development of habitats in the Post-glacial". Reprinted from: *Proc. Roy. Soc.*, **B161**, pp. 293–375.

Pigott, C. D. (1956). "The vegetation of Upper Teesdale in the north Pennines". *J. Ecol.*, **44**, pp. 545–586.

Vegetation and Man

Clarke, Grahame (1941). *Prehistoric England.* Batsford, 116 pp.

Cole, Sonia (1963). *The Neolithic Revolution.* British Museum, 66 pp.

Curwen, E. Cecil (1927). "Prehistoric Agriculture in Britain". *Antiquity*, **1**, pp. 261–289.

Darby, H. C. (1936). *Historical Geography of England before 1800.* Cambridge, 566 pp.

Hoskins, W. G. (1955). *The Making of the English Landscape.* Hodder, 240 pp.

Hoskins, W. G. (1967). *Fieldwork in Local History.* Faber & Faber, 192 pp.

Iversen, J. (1949). "The Influence of Prehistoric Man on Vegetation". *Geologica Survey of Denmark.* N. series **3**, No. 6, 25 pp.

Mitchell, G. F. (1965). "Littleton Bog, Tipperary: an Irish Agricultural Record". *Journ. Roy. Soc. Antiquaries of Ireland*, **95**, pp. 121–132.
Oldfield, F. (1963). "Pollen-analysis and man's role in the ecological history of the south-east Lake District". *Geografiska Annaler.*, *XLV*.
Richmond, I. A. (Ed.) (1961). *Roman and Native in North Britain*. Nelson, 174 pp. Chap. I by Stuart Piggot.
Turner, J. (1964). "The anthropogenic factor in vegetational History. I. Tregaron and Whixall Mosses". *New Phytologist*, **63**, pp. 73–90.
Turner, J. (1965). "A contribution to the history of forest clearance". *Proc. Roy. Soc.*, **B161**, pp. 343–354.

Present British flora and vegetation

Darling, Fraser and Boyd, Morton (1964). "The Highlands and Islands". *New Naturalist*, Collins, 336 pp.
Burnett, J. H. (Ed.) (1964). *Vegetation of Scotland*. Oliver & Boyd, 613 pp.
Iversen, J. (1964). "Retrogressive vegetational succession in the post-Glacial". *J. Ecol.*, **52** (Suppl.), p. 59.
Ivimey-Cook, R. B. and Proctor, M. C. F. (1966). "The plant communities of the Burren, Co. Clare". *Proc. Roy. Irish Acad.*, **B64**, pp. 211–302.
Matthews, J. (1955). *Origin and Distribution of the British Flora*. Hutchinson, 176 pp.
McVean, D. N. and Ratcliffe, D. A. (1962). "Plant Communities of the Scottish Highlands". *Monographs of the Nature Conservancy*: Number One.
Pearsall, W. H. (1950). "Mountains and Moorlands". *New Naturalist*, Collins, 312 pp.
Ratcliffe, D. A. and Walker, D. (1958). "The Silver Flowe, Galloway, Scotland." *J. Ecol.*, **46**, pp. 407–445.
Salisbury, E. J. (1961). "Weeds and Aliens". *New Naturalist*, Collins, 384 pp.
Tallis, J. H. (1964). "Studies on southern Pennine peats." *J. Ecol.*, **52**, pp. 323–353.
Walker, D. and Walker, P. M. (1961). "Stratigraphic evidence of regeneration in some Irish bogs." *J. Ecol.*, **49**, pp. 169–185.

Lake Sediments

Mackereth, F. J. H. (1966). "Some chemical observation on post-glacial lake sediments." *Phil. Trans. Roy. Soc.* **B250**, pp. 165–213.

Former Forests

Lamb, H. H. (1964). "Trees and climatic history in Scotland." *Q. J. Roy Met. Soc.*, **90**, pp. 382–394.

Glossary

AEROBIC—describing either organisms which require oxygen to live, or conditions where oxygen is present.

ANAEROBIC—describing either organisms which flourish in the absence of oxygen, or conditions where oxygen is absent.

BASE—in the chemical sense, a substance which neutralises an acid.

BASE-RICH—of a soil, one containing much lime or potash.

BLANKET-BOG—an area of peat which is not confined to a basin, but covers ground of moderate slope.

BROWN-EARTH—the characteristic soil type under deciduous forest in N.W. Europe, in which the humus is of the mull type and well mixed with the topmost mineral soil.

COLLOIDAL CLAY—clay of a particle-size so small that it has distinctive physical properties.

CRAG—a shelly sediment formed under shallow marine conditions.

CRYOTURBATION—a type of frost disturbance of soils in which the visible layers of the soil profile become folded and otherwise contorted.

DRIFT—superficial deposits of mineral material which were carried and dropped by an ice-sheet.

ERRATIC—a stone or boulder of a rock foreign to the site on which it is found, indicating transport by ice from an area where that rock outcrops.

FEN—a swampy area where the ground water-level reaches the surface, and a peat which is not acid has accumulated.

FORAMINIFERA—a group of minute animals (Protozoa) of the marine plankton, having calcareous shells.

INTERGLACIAL—an interval between two glaciations during which the temperature rose at least as high as during the Post-glacial period.

INTERSTADIAL—a climatic fluctuation within a glacial period, of smaller magnitude than an interglacial.

KETTLE-HOLE—a hollow in glacial debris formed by the melting of a block of dead ice.

LEACHING—solution and removal of minerals from a soil by rainwater.

MOR—an acid soil humus which accumulates at the soil surface, and is too acid for the presence of earthworms.

MORAINE—in English, a mound or ridge formed of till. An irregular type of hummocky moraines, formed by groups of mounds with intervening deep hollows, is sometimes called "kettle-moraine" and interpreted as the deposit left by ice which melted *in situ*; persistent blocks of dead ice melted later than the rest, forming the hollows. Ridge moraines have usually been formed as terminal, lateral, or medial moraines to a valley glacier.

MULL—a fertile soil humus, not acid, and well mixed with the superficial layer of mineral soil; inhabited by earthworms.

OMBROGENOUS—peat which lies above the ground water-level, so that plants on its surface depend on rainwater for their supply of minerals.

PODSOL—a soil type in which there is a surface layer of acid humus and below this a severely leached mineral layer; typically found under coniferous forest and heaths.

RAISED BOG—a peat bog developed on a level substratum and having the form of a dome, the peat being thickest at the centre of the bog, so that the surface is convex.

RECURRENCE SURFACE—a change in the type of peat in a bog profile, from dark highly humified and presumably slow-growing peat, to fresh unhumified and much faster-growing peat; interpreted as indicating an increase in humidity.

REGENERATION COMPLEX—the assemblage of plants which formed the vegetation of the newly wet bog surface and gave rise to the fresh peat immediately above a Recurrence Surface—i.e. when the bog surface was "regenerated" by increased humidity.

SOLIFLUCTION—the flowing or creeping of soil down a slope which occurs in cold climates as a result of alternate freezing and thawing of the soil water.

TILL—Boulder clay. The unsorted mineral debris carried by an ice sheet.

TOPOGENOUS PEAT—peat formed in drainage basins which receive ground water from a land surface.

TUFF—a fine-grained igneous rock, sometimes with cleavage properties resembling those of flint.

Index

Hunstanton, 27
Hypnum, 81

Ilex aquifolium (Holly), 16, 102, 103, 104
Insect remains, 17, 28–30
Interglacial, definition of, 14
— vegetation cycle, 14, 61
"Intermediate terrace" of River Cam, 26
Interstadial, definition of, 25–6
Ipswich, 17
Ipswichian Interglacial, 13, 16, 17, 20,
    21, 22, 25, 26, 85, 112
Ireland, 6, 16, 34, 41, 46, 49, 50, 51, 52,
    55, 56, 58, 59, 65, 70, 71, 74, 78, 79, 81,
    84, 98, 102, 114, 116, 120–24, 126–7,
    130, 133, 135, 138
Iris pseudacorus, 119
Irish Sea, 28, 36
— vegetation history, 76, 86–7
Iron Age, 72, 75, 81, 86, 88, 89, 90, 92,
    98, 105
Iversen, J., 33, 35, 40, 42, 43, 50, 64–5,
    70, 71, 72, 86
Ivy (*Hedera helix*), 57, 58, 64–6, 107

Jack-by-the-hedge, 99
Jasione, 36
Jessen, K., 34, 37
Johnson, G. A. L., 86, 125
Juglans (Walnut), 8
Juncus alpinus, 110
Juniperus communis (Juniper), 30, 34, 35,
    39, 40, 42, 43, 44, 45, 102, 107, 109,
    124

Kent, 78
Kerney, M. P., 78
Keskadale Oaks, 104
Kobresia simpliciuscula, 110
Koeleria, 110, 111
Koenigia islandica, 36, 40, 54, 130, 132
Kroskienko, 3, 8

"lagg", of a raised bog, 121
Lake District, 27, 39, 41, 66, 74, 75, 79,
    82, 83, 84, 86, 94, 98, 100, 102, 122,
    130

Lambert, C. A., 26
Landnam, 70–4, 76, 103, 104
Langdale Pikes, 73
Larix decidua (Larch), 100
Late Bronze Age trackways, 70, 81–2
Late-glacial period (Late-Weichselian),
    24, 26, 32–41, 59, 90, 91, 101,
    108, 110, 127, 130, 133
— vegetation, 24, 31–40, 50, 108, 110,
    113, 114, 130, 133
Lea Valley Arctic beds, 3, 27
Leaching, 61–2, 86, 112
Ligustrum vulgare, 99
Lime (*Tilia*), 51, 55, 56, 57, 58, 59, 66,
    75, 83, 84, 102
Ling (*Calluna*), 13, 61, 80, 111
Liriodendron, 8
Little Woodbury, 92–3
Llyn Idwal, 113–14
Loch Clair, 45
— Droma, 27, 39–40
— Maree, 41, 45, 62, 96
— Sionascaig, 40, 51, 62, 106
Lochan nan Cat, 56
Lodgepole Pine, 100
London Clay, 3, 4, 6
— — flora, 7, 8
Lowestoft Glaciation, 3, 14, 15, 16, 21
    (now Anglian)
— Till, 14, 15 (now Anglian)
Ludham, 11, 12, 15, 21
Ludhamian temperate period, 12, 21
Lüneburg Heath, 36, 110, 127
Lusitanian element in the Irish flora,
    16, 46, 50, 135
Lycopodium clavatum, 108
— *selago*, 36, 108

Macroscopic plant remains, 5, 25, 29,
    57, 102
MacVean, D. N., 113
— and Ratcliffe, D. A., 125
Maglemosian site, 55
Magnolia, 7, 8
— *cor*, 10
Mammoth, 29, 30
Marks Tey, 15, 16, 17